HOW TO GET PUBLICITY

HOW TO GET PUBLICITY

And Make the Most of It
* Once You've Got It *

WILLIAM PARKHURST

Times BOOKS

All rights reserved under International and Pan-American Copyright Conventions. Published in the United States by Times Books, a division of Random House, Inc., New York, and simultaneously in Canada by Random House of Canada Limited, Toronto.

Library of Congress Cataloging in Publication Data

Parkhurst, William.
  How to get publicity (and make the most of it once you've got it).

  Bibliography: p. 233
  Includes index.
  1. Public relations. 2. Industrial publicity.
I. Title.
HD59.P353   1985   659.2   84–40435
ISBN 0-8129-1161-X

Designed by Doris Borowsky

Manufactured in the United States of America
9 8 7 6 5 4 3 2 1

First Edition

To Molly

Acknowledgments

The author is greatly indebted to the following media professionals for their assistance in compiling this book: Emily Boxer, Steve Friedman, and Marty Ryan of *Today*; Bob Dolce of the *Tonight Show*; Patricia McMillen of *Donahue*; Landon Y. Jones of *Money*; G.H. Simpson of *Newsweek*; and Don Hewitt of *Sixty Minutes*.

There is no way to express my appreciation for the publicity professionals who took the time to share their views, materials, and even office space while the book was being written: Sandee Brawarsky, Times Books; Diane Glynn, Diane Glynn Publicity and Public Relations, Inc.; Donna Gould, Donna Gould Associates; Barbara J. Hendra, Barbara J. Hendra Associates; Mike Levine and Rich Frishman, Planned Television Arts Ltd.; and Melissa Lande, M.L. Promotions, Inc.

Technical advice was greatly appreciated from David Weinstein, Cinema Sound Studios; Steve Dworkin, Cue Recording; John Sullivan and Tom Tucker, Public Affairs Satellite System, Inc.; Bill Hufnagle and Rochelle Barkas, Vidlo Productions, Inc.; and cinematographers Jerry Cartwell and Vincent Still.

Special thanks go to authors Dan Greenburg and Suzanne

O'Malley for telling me touring-author stories during a radio interview on WOR, New York; to Tania Grossinger for her contributions to the "Publicity at Work" chapter; to Chris Katz for the "inverted pyramid"; and to Bill Hewitt for his support and help.

Sarah Parsons of Times Books kept track of me and the manuscript, and my final acknowledgment is reserved for Kathleen Moloney, my editor, who went far beyond the usual encouragement and support of the project. She said the nicest words a first-time author can hear: "Let's do the book."

Contents

Introduction

"I'm very impressed with what I've seen of your work, Mr. Parkhurst. But frankly, there are—gaps."

I was applying for a position as an industrial public relations consultant, and I was not enjoying the interview. As far as I was concerned, the only gaps came with this guy's tendency to pause meaningfully as he tried to see into my soul. In my fifteen years of experience, I had publicized my mother's yard sale; I had conducted a press conference for the admiral in charge of the nation's entire Naval Reserve program; I had worked in a corporate environment where part of my job was to get grilled by investigative reporters; and I had booked myself on tour as a spokesman for a nonprofit organization. Most of my more ambitious campaigns had been done in book publishing, where I publicized *The Total Woman* and Joey the Hit Man the same year. Gaps I felt I didn't have.

My interviewer was still explaining. "You see, it's all well and good when you're working with people, but I don't see where you have anything in your background that would relate to a piece of plastic."

He took another pause.

3

"That's what you do here? Publicize pieces of plastic?" I asked.

"That's right, and I'm not talking about interesting plastic, the kind *anyone* could publicize." I was getting the impression that he had made this speech before. "I'm talking," he said, "about the *resins* that make up plastic. How would you publicize a resin, Mr. Parkhurst?"

The man was right. There were gaps. And today, five years later, there still are. I have never publicized a resin.

But I have tried everything in this book, including the "new stuff"—distribution of release material to radio, television, and cable by satellite. In fact, that's my specialty these days. I have also seen some amazing results from other people in publicity. I met an executive of a multinational PR firm who used publicity to sell tons of avocados after there had been an overabundant harvest, a success story that affected nothing less than the economy of California that year. I saw someone use publicity to put a disease on an episode of *Marcus Welby, M.D.* in the early seventies, when it was the hottest show on television. Ten thousand talking-head interviews couldn't have done the cause more good than that single, prime-time hour on a Tuesday night did. I know someone who travels free whenever and wherever she wants because the hotel chains know that she will appear on local talk shows, drop a few brand names, and send the tapes to the home office. I have a friend who bartered services with a couple of nice guys who installed excellent burglar alarm systems in New York. I thought this person was making a mistake. "Publicize burglar alarm systems in New York? But it's so *overdone*," said I.

To help a friend, I booked the two installers on my Manhattan cable show, figuring that would be about the best publicity they would receive. It is impossible to describe the number of "home security" features there had been in New York. The subject had to be closed.

But this person, like all of the very best publicity practitioners, is an artist. These two cheerful alarm people from Queens were soon profiled in *The New York Times* and *The Wall Street Journal*, on local news programs, and in virtually every choice placement in a town that hates to book anyone with less glitter than Princess Di. For the thousandth time I realized that the only limits that can be put on a publicity campaign are those seated in our own negative thinking.

In the following pages, you'll see what I mean. You'll learn to reach the media for purposes you never believed were possible. You will soon know how to expand business or career opportunities, to promote a cause, to build and enhance a public image, to enjoy the satisfaction of increased stature in your home or work community.

You'll also learn how to employ media as a competitive tool in beating a rival to the account, stopping the interstate from passing through your living room, or increasing corporate visibility through coverage in trade journals. You'll discover how to hold a press conference, handle an adversary interview, and arrange a photo session.

You will learn what it takes to appear on network programs and how to travel the beaten-path tour circuit taken by famous people for promotional purposes for more than fifty years. And there is advice on planning your campaign, and guidelines that will enable you to produce materials likely to pique press interest and prepare you to let out the public side of your personality.

All books that give advice start with an annoying pep talk that emphasizes diligence and the importance of not getting discouraged early on. This one has six parts:

1. *Publicity requires work.* Communicating your message will require a strong commitment coupled with a new approach to your view of radio, television, cable, and print. It will demand a self-critique at every stage of your progress.

2. *Press resistance to your efforts is a way of life.* It should not be confused with its distant cousin, personal rejection. The temptation to console yourself with the "contacts are everything" rationalization will be very strong, sometimes overwhelming. But when you persist, publicity always materializes.

3. *Publicity will probably not make you famous.* If fame is your goal, close the book now, before you spill coffee on the pages, and give it away as a present. You will, of course, taste some of celebrity's magic nectar—but household words and their manufacture are beyond our intention.

4. *You won't have to do all publicity chores by yourself.* You may, for example, wish to enlist a friend to help with making your telephone calls or writing your press releases. Initially, though, you should do your own backstage work to get the feel of all facets of publicity and to fortify a habit of assuming the total responsibility that should always underscore your campaign.

5. *You already know much more than you think about publicity and the media.* After all, you've been watching television, listening to the radio, and reading since you were a kid. You already have an idea of what compels you to trust someone.

6. *Publicity takes time.* Progress in publicity is exhilarating, a high that transcends any drug. You may be tempted to skip a few rungs, especially when you see someone on national television or in *People* magazine with less to offer than you. But don't skip any steps. In publicity, what appears to be the long way around usually is not.

Since you're reading this book, you've probably pictured yourself on the talk-show couch and even rehearsed what you might say. You've seen the words of an article written about you, and maybe you've even worked out your pose in an accompanying photograph. Continue developing those images and strengthening them daily, because your efforts, with some help from this book, will give you the opportunity to speak your piece. Shyness is no liability, as any famous person will tell you. We're all shy, but there's a ham inside us begging for a little limelight.

While it would be absurd to downplay either the specialized knowledge of public relations professionals or the value of contacts in getting an idea across, publicity can be done as a do-it-yourself project; what's more, it can be a lot easier than building a picnic table. Those high school English lessons on writing business letters will pay off at last. A typewriter, notebook, cassette recorder, telephone, and an initial fortification of patience and persistence are the only tools you need to begin advancing personal goals through publicity. You are going to be very surprised at what the media will be able to do for you.

1

Publicity: What It Is and Isn't

Before you embark on the road to publicity, you'll need a few definitions and a few eye-opening facts.

Publicity is the garnering of free media exposure for promotional purposes, an uncomplicated concept with many moving parts. Advertising is the spending of money for commercial exposure. It's a short message, and goes right for the monetary jugular. You get what you pay for. If you want to sell your car or get the word out on a dress sale, advertising is your best shot, because the press does not give away time or space that should rightly be sold.

But suppose the car is a forty-year-old Chrysler restored to its original splendor. Suppose also that you're able to trace its history through two generations of ownership. Now you have the car that saw the end of the Great Depression, the horror of World War II, the rise of television, the Beatles, Vietnam, Watergate . . . and through it all the machine was driven and loved by an assortment of interesting people whose snapshots tell a story. The car is no longer a vehicle on the market, but a testament to yesterday. It becomes a candidate for enhanced salability through publicity.

Let's look again at those dresses sitting in the boutique wait-

8

ing for either moths or customers to take them away. Their only history is that they didn't sell. The shop owner frowns and takes what appears to be her only option—advertising them at 25 percent off and trying to figure out a business where perfectly fashionable attire hasn't caught on locally.

Suddenly, a small item in the newspaper changes the shop owner's perspective. The mayor's wife is looking for merchants to donate time and goods for an annual charity fund raiser at the country club. *Everyone* will be there. The shop owner calls and offers to donate one dress that represents a new mode of fashion being displayed in boutiques from New York to Los Angeles, while offering the rest for a fashion show. The town's most prominent women are persuaded to pose as models, the local newspaper takes photographs, and the dresses move at their original prices within two days.

In both examples, an advertising chore became a publicity story because of an *angle*. Whether it's called a news peg, slant, hook, or handle, the angle is the story's foundation and the pivotal element of a publicity campaign, however large or small.

Angles are derived from the journalist's time-honored news litany: Who? What? When? Where? Why? and How? With varying emphasis, these six questions carry a subliminal, subjective "pricing code" that editors use to determine the timeliness and suitability of an idea.

In Chapter 4, you'll learn more about using the five W's and the H. For now, keep asking yourself *who* you are, *what* you're doing, *when* you're doing it (if applicable), *where* you're doing it, and where people will be affected, *why* it matters, and *how* you get it done. Observe news stories to see which of these building blocks lead the emphasis and which are excluded altogether.

If you look closely, you'll be able to see angles all around you. Take a notebook and begin jotting down angles as you see them in broadcasting and print. Work at spotting the news and feature value of ordinary objects and events.

Sometimes, you'll notice that there is no realistic angle. The dresses might be so ugly that no town councilwoman would model them in a fashion show, and the car might be a rusty nine-year-old sedan with bald tires. In such cases, advertise and be done with the project. It's the most efficient way out.

The entries in your notebook that point out the nonstories are as vital as the ones that analyze legitimate news angles. It's wonderful to exercise imagination, but no one can create a publicity story when there is insufficient Who, What, When, Where, Why, and How. The press can be lured, coaxed, and occasionally seduced into doing you a favor on borderline ideas, but blatant manipulation is out. Media people have a keen eye for a story; when one isn't there, badgering them will only alienate them.

Tens of millions of dollars' worth of media exposure is given away in this country every day. That statement has the unsettling ring of a matchbook-cover land deal or a mail-order doctorate, but if you take the published advertising rate data and apply it to the amount of time you spend on the air, or the amount of space given to you by a print source, you begin to get a sense of publicity's worth. Suppose *Sixty Minutes* does a thirteen-minute feature on your business on a Sunday, when its advertising is worth $500,000 for a half-minute. Or suppose you do seven minutes on the *Tonight Show* on a routine week night, when the show's sponsors are paying $30,000 for a half-minute of time. Arithmetic gives us a value of $13 million for your appearance on *Sixty Minutes* and $420,000 for bantering with Johnny and Ed.

Publicity time, however, has a value beyond published advertising rates, because you are part of the programming and not just an excuse to run to the refrigerator for a snack.

There are 4,857 commercial AM radio stations, 4,500 radio, television, and cable talk shows, 3,421 commercial FM stations, 1,252 noncommercial FMs, 541 commercial VHF television stations, 473 commercial UHF TV outlets, 117 noncommercial VHFs, 189 noncommercial UHFs, 5,000 cable systems, 1,699 daily newspapers, and more than 5,000 magazines in the United States. We have 50 newly minted radio networks, with twice that many television and cable networks on—or about to go on—the air. Most of the cable systems have not yet begun their conversion to a 50- or 100-channel capability, and the nation is only 35 percent wired.

In 1982, the Federal Communications Commission (FCC) authorized the construction of an additional 5,000 low-power television stations that will soon begin serving urban areas with a capacity to snatch signals directly from satellites, bypassing cable altogether.

In space, new satellites are put into geosynchronous orbit 23,500 miles above the equator as rapidly as space shuttles can be launched to carry them. These "birds" already mean that any of us can start an ad hoc network with a technical capability of reaching all fifty states; we can do so for a few thousand dollars. The fact that such a project can be undertaken for so little money is a testament to a new age that confounds even science-fiction writers.

What all this means to civilization is something for mediaphiles and behavioral scientists to debate into the twenty-first century. What it means to us is that we have an opportunity to prosper from the expansion, to employ the media as a tool for personal, professional, and financial growth.

People believe that producers and editors are too busy to take telephone calls and that their feature ideas spring exclusively from their staffs, but they're wrong. Assignment editors and producers know that hard news such as bombings in Beirut and SALT talks aren't enough to sustain ratings and subscription levels. They need a large supply of human-interest stories, and usually they don't object if these stories are punctuated with promotional tie-ins in the form of plugs.

The small number of people who profit from their industry knowledge would like you to believe that contacts are everything—that no one gets on the *Donahue* show without an in of some kind and that a *Sixty Minutes* segment comes from drinking with major-league journalists. Untrue.

Most feature material, and even some hard news, focuses on workaday citizens going about their business. They don't have clout, but they do have a story to tell. Corporations and special-interest groups might control real estate and politicians, but they have never controlled the press. It is ours. As difficult as the notion is to grasp at times, it is critical to our process that you remind yourself of your right of access. The press is open to the public and will probably be interested in what you have to say.

Public relations (PR) is the genus of publicity, the parental umbrella of media and image-centered activities that include speech writing, policy statements, preparation for journalists' questions, syndication of prepared articles, and even the canning of broadcast interviews offered to radio, television, and cable as public-affairs interviews.

PR people are media mercenaries who espouse a particular product or cause. We're familiar with the image of the strip-mining company spokesman trying to keep *Sixty Minutes* away from the door. Lately, however, we're more likely to see that person inviting Mike Wallace inside and taking the questions, looking the interviewer in the eye, and firmly stating that the arsenic that seeped into the community's drinking water was someone else's fault. There are Wallace surrogates in public relations firms who rehearse such scenarios with executives, doing so with a brutality that makes the real thing seem almost a relief.

The practice is not as seamy as it might appear. The press has its own excesses and the advantage of being able to splice. In cases where an investigative piece assaults a company unfairly, the result can be disastrous, with exonerating litigation taking years. A strong case with a spokesman as comfortable under the heat of the lights as the reporter is more democratic and far less expensive.

Not that public relations people are up there with Mother Teresa in terms of good works, but they are sometimes the victims of a snide uttering that something "sounds like a lot of PR," an implication that those in the field are launderers of the truth. Most PR people, if only for pragmatic reasons, won't lie to the press or represent a client who asks them to do so.

Spokesmen for asbestos, Agent Orange, or tobacco are more visible than their counterparts in less controversial industries. During the Tylenol crisis of 1982, public relations personnel worked long shifts and helped assure people that the medication they took for this morning's headache wouldn't kill them. In times of assassination, natural disaster, rumors of war, and every type of public crisis, the spokesman we see translating jargon into English in front of all those microphones is a public relations person doing a job.

Our focus is on personal publicity, where you have something to say, you're excited about it, you take to the media, and you benefit from the exposure. Besides the misconception that contacts are the be-all and end-all of the process, here are a few other misconceptions:

You need a super sales personality.   No way. High-powered hypers who think they can bulldoze their way into the green room of a talk show get a backstage reputation that works against them. Polite sincerity, conviction, and an understanding of the show's programming needs will carry you all the way.

You need to be a communications expert.   You need to listen to the radio, watch television, and read newspapers and magazines, but you need no special media or communications expertise.

You need charisma to appear on television.   The charisma that got you your job, dates, sports trophies, or the part in the school play is enough. Naturally, you'll have to work hard on developing your public side, but unless you want Phil Donahue's job, charisma is not anything to worry about.

You must have something newsworthy to get exposure.   Interesting, yes; newsworthy, no. If you're doing something that actually makes hard news, you'll know it without making so much as a phone call. The press will camp on your lawn until you come out. Otherwise, anything interesting will have an audience.

You need a public relations or communications background to target your campaign through the nation's talk-show matrix. That wouldn't hurt, but a few computerized reference texts from the library will do. Chapter 27 tells you what they are.

You need a sophisticated writing style.   The clear use of language is imperative, but the intricacies of advanced creative writing can actually be a hindrance. Journalists have discarded slickness in favor of a straightforward writing style that minimizes adjectives and florid elements of construction. If you forgot your grammar after high school, you'll either have to bone up or find a friend to help you with the written materials. You'll need a typewriter that doesn't smudge and an eye for detail. There can be no errors, cross-outs, or other tip-offs to amateurism.

You have to know about camera angles, makeup, and other techniques.   Watching television carefully is more important than any of the above. We'll show you the basics of studio presence in future chapters.

You need public-speaking experience.   In publicity, oratorial speech is not necessary; somewhat more polished conversational speech is what you'll be aiming for. You're supposed to have some fear of speaking in public—everyone is terrified at times. Apprehension generally evolves into a major asset. So will your cassette recorder.

Publicity is not a panacea. Many people subscribe to a mistaken belief that shouting loud enough and long enough guarantees the success of a project. You should know about some of publicity's limitations.

Publicity will not make you a star. De Niro, Streep, and Hoffman ultimately made it on their own acting ability, Jagger and Pavarotti on their ability to communicate through their music. Publicity will take you to the people, but only they can decide if they want you to be a celebrity and, if so, for how long.

Publicity will sell nothing unless people want it. You may choose not to believe that point—quote P. T. Barnum and fondle your aging pet rock—but somewhere along the way, you'll come to believe it. Something has to click for people to buy.

Publicity has nothing to do with stunts. The word *publicity* is often coupled with the word *stunt*, but the alliance is about as contemporary as cars that start with cranks. Press agents emeriti will recall the good old days when New York had half a dozen daily newspapers and more columnists than anyone could count, when Hedda Hopper or Walter Winchell could start a sales landslide with a few short lines about a staged promotional event. Today's PR professional generally ignores stunts, because they do not work. They can also backfire, leaving the client with an embarrassing set of negative clippings that linger in the collective subconscious for years. They are best left to experienced specialists who understand how to make them work.

Our final note on what publicity isn't. It isn't—or need not be—expensive. Occasionally, one encounters a sleazoid who says, "For five hundred, I can grease a few palms and get you on the show. Money talks in this world, pal." Take a hike, pal. Radio, television, and cable exist under the scrutiny of the Federal Communications Commission, the government agency empowered to yank their licenses. The Federal Trade Commission (FTC) is empowered to prosecute broadcast or print enterprises if anything doesn't look good. There are sanctions, guilds, codes of ethics everywhere. Your campaign won't cost you much. You should plan on getting between a thousand and a million dollars' worth of exposure for little more than petty cash.

Let's get started.

2
Getting Started

The first three things you need are a television set, a radio, and a notebook. You might prefer a steno pad with a line down the middle of each page, a wirebound job, a looseleaf, or even a file folder for storing random bits of paper. You need only be sure that you place notes where you can find them easily, because the scribbling you do now will be of great use later.

You're about to take on a dot-connecting exercise of watching television, listening to the radio, and reading as much as possible, to find the publicity behind interviews. A flu that traps you in the house with nothing to do is a plus, or you might just steal a day from work.

You need to start observing interview programming with a clinical, cynical view of why people are on the air talking about themselves. Consult your television and cable listings for talk shows, and start making appointments with yourself to be there when they're on. If you own a videotape recorder, you have the advantage of setting it to record particular programs for viewing at your convenience.

Most of us see television during the prime viewing hours of eight to eleven P.M., when the slickest entertainment shows are on. With very few exceptions, these hours represent the segment of the broadcast day of least interest to your publicity campaign. Begin watching on the opposite side of the day, with the national morning shows—*The CBS Morning News, Today,* and *Good Morning America.*

Set up your notebook as a log, following the sample for headings on the next page.

Now start to watch television, paying close attention to what is actually being sold and how the topic of the interview keys into it. You'll notice that few guests appear on these talk shows because they're eager to engage in scintillating discussions. Most television talk segments run between four and seven minutes, with the interviewer discharging the plug responsibility at the beginning and the end of the conversation. Frequently, there will be words on the screen below the guest's chin that mention a book, organization, movie, or whatever. This lettering is called a lower third, because of its place on the screen, and it quickens the pace of a discussion while serving as a plug.

Soon, you may start to wonder if *anyone* goes on the air just to talk. The comic has an upcoming appearance in Vegas. The singer just happens to be releasing a new album this week. The head of General Motors is there to talk about his fall lineup of Chevys.

Watch the shows for their formats as well as for the guest lineup. Notice that Phil Donahue's audience is as much a part of the program as he is, and that his show is confined to a single topic or guest each morning. *Today, CBS Morning News,* and *Good Morning America* offer the most glamorous guests between 7:30 and 8:00, when the ratings are up and the competition among them is keenest.

A program's commercials will tell you much about the demographic composition of its audience. The big advertising agencies have done your market research for you; you won't see denture-cream commercials anywhere near cartoons, and video games aren't likely to be sold during Lawrence Welk.

After exploring the network talk shows, check out those on your local stations. If you live near a large city, you'll find

Date	Time	Program	Station	Guest	Interviewer	Segment Length	Plug
6/17	7:45 A.M.	*Today*	WNBC-TV	Sylvester Stallone	Jane Pauley	5 minutes	*Staying Alive* (film)

After structuring at least ten pages in this format, prepare another ten as follows:

Date	Subject	Publication	Reporter	Words/Lines	Photograph	Plug
6/17	Dr. Robert Durant, chiropractic medicine	*Hillsboro Magazine*	George Jeffers	3,000 words	Yes	His practice

many of the same stars who appeared on the nationals nodding
politely as less-sophisticated interviewers carefully enunciate
the plugs. These name guests are on tour and frequently spend
weeks in the major markets talking away. Quite often, the host
will have to cut the interview short so that the star can dash
across town to do another show. Pay particular attention to the
guests who follow the celebrity, the people whose emphasis is
more local. You may soon be among them.

Your start in television will probably not be on a daily talk
show in a major market, but on a Sunday morning public affairs interview with a name like *Focus, Viewpoint, Perspective, Today in Tuscaloosa,* or *Community.* Check *TV Guide*
and the newspaper for programs that seem to fit this category.
They often aren't important enough to warrant the customary
three lines of description. You may have come across one of
these shows when fate put you near the set at an ungodly hour
of a weekend morning, and you probably wondered why they
are on the air.

They are on because the government requires stations to
come up with regular programming that's supposed to serve
the needs of surrounding communities. Sometimes these
public-affairs shows are surprisingly good, hosted by a member of the station's news team, or perhaps by a clergyman with
a little vaudeville under the collar. More often, they're awful.
The good news is that they're always there.

Watch as many of these public-affairs shows as you can
stand, adding the even less professional local cable programming to your agenda if possible. While broadcasters have to
give away a little time to the public, cablecasters frequently
are forced to turn over entire *channels* to their communities.
Anyone can get on the air, as either guest or host, and practice
in a talk-show environment.

Radio is next. Start with a polished program such as *The
Larry King Show.* It may keep you up all night, but you'll
learn a lot about radio's unique luxury of having time to cover

topics and promote a guest. Again, every guest seems to be selling something.

The nearest big-city talk stations will provide a view of the sophistication and planning of talk radio. Hosts are often specialized—psychologists, sportscasters, lawyers, and political interviewers are carefully chosen to suit their station's audience at a given time of day. As you take your notes, begin to picture yourself on these shows and start thinking about what you'll say. After the big-city talkers come the local live shows, where the hosts are less specialized and rely on the telephone for audience participation. Next are the radio counterparts of the same public-affairs spokespeople you watched on television. Radio operates under its own FCC rules; programmers have to be open to program suggestions from their listeners.

Read every newspaper that serves your community—dailies, weeklies, special-interest publications, shopping guides with features—anything that might be promising to your campaign. The possibilities of print are at least as interesting as your broadcast options, perhaps even more so.

Magazines are an ongoing, comprehensive part of your research. *Read them all the time.* Start with those you enjoy most and comb the newsstands for city and county magazines, journals, whatever your message should appear in. *Time, Newsweek,* and other newsmagazines should be watched very carefully, for they expand the definition of news to every aspect of our culture. When something has been promoted well enough to have caught on, you'll read about it as a news item. When you fly, take the airline's magazine home.

All coverage is important. Even those little radio, TV, and cable public-affairs shows are endowed with clout beyond belief. You'll notice that they have evangelists of every denomination as neighbors in their obscure time slots, whose shows end with a solicitation of some kind.

When the religious pitches come from a distant city, you're probably listening to a "program-length commercial," where

the church has *purchased* the air time from the station. The
clergymen know something most of us don't. Broadcast evan-
gelism of this kind, operating from the same black holes of the
broadcast schedules as public-affairs shows, brings megabucks
to the sponsoring missions. There is no such thing as dead time
or wasted space in the media. It's all profitable to someone.

③

Setting Your Primary Campaign Goal

An ancient pep talk on direction says that if you don't know where you're going, you're probably not going to get there. In publicity, eliminate the "probably." You need to be very specific about what you want from the campaign, or your interviews will be a mere narcissistic ride. It's a good idea to list possible objectives and take note of a dominating theme. Here are a few guidelines:

Be realistic.   Choose a goal that assumes no big breaks through national exposure. There is a virtual certainty of local and regional coverage, however, and you should pace yourself on the basis of that assumption.

Be very specific.   Treat your primary campaign goal like a fraction reduced to its lowest common denominator. You'll be expected to hold your own on a variety of related topics, but when it comes time to go to the cashier's window for the plug, you should be selling only one thing.

Choose with your personality in mind.   It may be that your firm specializes in the sale of municipal bonds but you're more interested in a lucrative subspecialty, the sheltering of taxable income through oil and gas exploration ventures. Go with the oil and gas.

Choose with your audience in mind. No one is required to pay attention to you. But if you excite an audience, they will never leave. Let us say that you are excited about oil and gas tax shelters, and the street smarts that made you successful at selling them tell you to avoid the legalese in favor of a simple starting point: You will tell them how to make a lot of money fast. You maintain your rapport by keeping your topic of discussion at a level the audience will understand. They will follow you anywhere.

Here are a few examples that should help in setting your goals.

You're a dentist who wants to expand a general practice, and you make a notation accordingly:

PRIMARY CAMPAIGN GOAL: Expansion of practice.

Your goal is short and to the point. You're ready for the next step. However, you start to think about dentures and how much you dislike providing them for patients. You also love children but hate to see their sticky little hands on the arms of your chair. You begin to picture a campaign that brings legions of children and elderly people to your office. You don't want to reject them, but you're most comfortable with patients who need the new cosmetic techniques you learned about at a recent seminar. So you scratch out your notation (it's your notebook and you can do whatever you want to it) and you make a revised entry:

PRIMARY CAMPAIGN GOAL: Expansion of practice, especially in cosmetic dentistry.

You'll probably talk about everything from false teeth to root canal, but the plug, which is generally going to be in your control, will stress cosmetic work.

You're a thirty-year-old woman who has been flying since the age of fifteen. Your employer, Kankakee Air Charters, wants to see you drumming up some business. You discuss the emphasis of the campaign with the boss and decide that you're more likely to reach potential students than air charter customers. You write up your primary campaign goal as follows:

PRIMARY CAMPAIGN GOAL: Increased student volume.

Then you start to procrastinate. As you visualize the campaign, you begin to see articles in area newspapers and their headlines: PERT BLONDE PILOT TEACHES BEGINNERS HOW TO FLY; PRETTIEST PILOT IN ILLINOIS URGES EVERYONE TO HEAD SKYWARD; WOMAN PILOT SAYS LEARN TO FLY EARLY.

You see the accompanying photograph, which has you smiling from the left seat of a Cessna, a local Charlie's Angel without Farrah Fawcett's salary. You realize that being a woman pilot is a plus and you plan to use it as a secondary angle, but you have a vague uneasiness about the tenor of the approach.

It occurs to you that you don't want to be only pretty, pert, or an employee of Kankakee Air. You want to fly for an airline, a laurel that befits your training and experience. It's no secret with your boss—everyone who flies wants a shot at aviation's big time. You agree to go after the publicity and give assurances that Kankakee Air will be mentioned in every interview, but your notation is now different.

PRIMARY CAMPAIGN GOAL: To build a clipping portfolio that will help in getting an airline job.

Now suppose you're an auto mechanic. In the era of the
$15,000 Chevy, talk-show doors will be very open to you if you
can tell people how to choose a good mechanic, how to make
their own minor repairs, and what the common rip-offs of
your trade are. You own a garage, you want people to bring
their cars in, and you don't care what kind of work needs to be
done. You can handle it all. Your notation looks like this:

PRIMARY CAMPAIGN GOAL: To get people into Art's
Texaco.

You're all set, Art. In the next chapter, you'll find out what
your booking angles are, you'll make your press kit and face the
world. But something's bothering you. You're losing business
when your customers buy European or Japanese cars, and
you're stuck with a prejudice that American garages can't handle the repair of these vehicles. You believe such an assumption
to be nonsense, and you're prepared to talk about it. Now you
have an amended notation:

PRIMARY CAMPAIGN GOAL: To get more people with
European and Japanese cars into Art's Texaco.

The primary campaign goal is simply the dominating purpose of your campaign. It is not an ironclad entity; change it
when you feel it isn't right. It will neither exclude other goals
nor serve as the sole topic of your interview conversation. Take
all the time you need to find it, however, because the primary
campaign goal is the start, finish, and bottom line of your publicity expedition.

Your Booking Angles

Angles are what you have to offer the media—what you have to talk about. Perhaps your primary angle is what you do, perhaps it is what you believe, or how you accomplish your work. Again we turn to journalism's barometric indicators of newsworthiness, Who, What, When, Where, Why, and How, to seek a pattern that applies to your background. Answer the questions under each of the six headings, and a profile of your booking potential will emerge.

1. WHO

- Who are you in your community?

- Did you star in local athletics or plays?

- Did you ever make news that people still remember, such as a rescue or a citation for community achievement?

- Is your family local news in itself?

- Who are you in your professional community?

- Have you done anything that made industry news?

- Who stands to benefit from what you have to say in interviews?

- Did anyone live, die, or make news because they did what you are selling or advocating?

- Who works with you and are they newsworthy in any way?

- Assuming that your story has an emphasis in one of journalism's five Ws and H, do you see yourself as a Who story?

2. WHAT

- What do you do?

- What event are you promoting, if any?

- What is the primary idea or product that you are selling?

- What have you achieved that makes you interesting?

- What can someone learn from you?

- What are the pitfalls of what you do?

- What are the trends that will shape the future of your work?

- What chain of events will occur if something in your field does not go according to plan?

- What is the origin of your work?

- Aside from what makes *you* interesting, what makes your *work* interesting?

3. WHEN

- When did you start doing what you do?

- When were you born?

- When does your product or event become effective?

- When does your own story start?
- When will changes resulting from your work occur?
- When can your audience see you or your product?
- When does the story of your product or idea begin?
- If your audience does what you tell them to, when can they expect a change?
- When should a story about you run, or does it matter?
- When does your offer expire and, if it does, when will it be available again?

4. WHERE

- Where are you from?
- Where do you work?
- Where can your idea or product be seen?
- Where is your project going to be most effective?
- Where is the local tie-in or distributor for your product or idea?
- Where is your event going to be held?
- Where are the people around you from?
- Where did you get your education or special training?
- Are there any additional local people or places that stand to benefit from what you do? If so, where are they?
- Where do you take it from here?

5. WHY

- Why do you do what you do?

- Why should anyone else do what you do?

- Why did you decide to pursue this line of thinking?

- Why do any of us need to learn more about it?

- Why do you make specific claims about your product or ideas?

- Why won't we be better off doing it another way?

- Why should your audience listen to you above any other expert in your field?

- Why did you decide to take your idea to the public through publicity appearances?

6. HOW

- How does it work?

- How do people get it?

- How easy is it for the average viewer in the audience?

- How long does it last?

- How good is it?

- How did you get where you are?

- How can someone else get there?

- How long did it take you to get there?

- How long can someone else expect to take getting there?

- How will it go wrong, if it does?

Returning to the notebook, set up your headings and list your angles. Your pattern should resemble the following example.

PRIMARY CAMPAIGN GOAL: Election to City Council.

Who:

Julie Anne McGrath, 22 Church St., Madison, NY. 42052

Born: Madison, 4/22/52

Attended Madison High, 1966–1970

Pitcher, women's softball team, state championship, 1970

Cheerleader, 1969–70

National Honor Society, elected May 1969

Attended Yale University, 1970–74

Yale Law School, 1974–77

Awarded J.D. degree, high honors, June 1977

Employed at McGrath, Wooten, & Bell law firm, September 1977 to present, senior partner since 1980

Daughter of former Madison mayor Michael McGrath

Niece of Robert O'Conner, former City Council president

What:

Plan to run for Madison City Council, District 5

Believe in lowering tax rate through bond issues and increase in cigarette, alcohol taxes

Believe in new elementary school for East Side

Believe in saving Harriman Park from urban renewal renovation plan currently before City Council

Believe in setting up special prosecutor to investigate dumping of chemicals in Woodstock River

Registered Democrat

When:

Will open campaign headquarters July 14

Will campaign through November 7 (Election Day is November 8)

Plan fund raiser August 9

Why:

Time for younger political leaders to become involved in Madison electoral process

"Old Boy Network" too comfortable in power

Something has to be done about taxes

Something has to be done about the river

East Side must have new elementary school to accommodate increased influx of families with young children in area

How:

Special prosecutor must be impartial, and grand jury investigation should follow on river pollution issue

Bond issue will offer investment incentive to citizens of Madison, who will be offered first refusal; primary aim is to lower taxes, which can be done (see position paper)

Will run a clean campaign with help from young-adult program

Expect endorsements from established political leaders

Publicity angles come in a variety of shapes and sizes, but they always fit into one of the journalistic categories. Don't be surprised if your situation seems not to fit into one or more of the slots. The important thing is that you now realize that you fit somewhere, that what you have to say is as important as the words of anyone else, and that you're now ready to consolidate your angles into a press release.

5

Writing a Release

A release is a summary of a project written in a journalistic format. It can, if an editor chooses, be printed or broadcast virtually without revision. In smaller newspapers, magazines, and radio stations, it is not uncommon for a release to run exactly as written by its originating source. In large metropolitan dailies or national magazines, of course, printing a handout in its original form is very rare.

Releases end up in the trash so often, whether they're read or not, that one sometimes wonders about their validity. The blizzard of paperwork that buries the desk of every media person every day assures that a two-page release mailed by itself, with no supporting telephone call or kit, will not do your cause a lot of good. Hoping publicity will result from such an anonymous approach is akin to planning where to park the Rolls-Royce you're going to buy when you win the lottery. But this lottery can be rigged in your favor.

Despite its short life in many quarters, the release will always be the most important document of your campaign. When a would-be interviewer agrees to "look at your materials," he or she will scan the release in less than a minute before making the judgment that will yield, or fail to yield, publicity.

Once the interview is agreed upon, the release becomes the spinal column of the press person's preparation.

Almost anyone can write a release. Forget about creativity, education, or long metaphoric treks through the essence of humanity. Forget about *writing* as you know it. If you *hate* to write or fear it the way many dread the dentist, you just might be in the right frame of mind. If you love the creative process, you won't necessarily be left out, but there may be a few things to unlearn. Either way, the greatest difficulty in release writing is a tendency to overcomplicate.

"KISS"

Those ink-stained editors who are caricature refugees from *The Front Page* have a long-standing acronym that they pass along to the earnest, Clark Kent types fresh from college and eager for The Big Story: KISS—meaning Keep It Simple, Stupid. Inelegant perhaps, and no one has used "stupid" as a term of endearment since VE Day, but it does sum up your mission as a release writer. A release is a miniature news article and should conform to the journalistic tradition of saying as much as possible in the shortest space with the plainest language.

OF PYRAMIDS AND INVERTED PYRAMIDS

Note the following newspaper story excerpt:

2 U.S. Warships Again Bombard
Artillery Batteries Outside Beirut*
By Thomas L. Friedman
Special to The New York Times

BEIRUT, Lebanon, Sept. 20—For a second day, two American

*From *The New York Times*, September 21, 1983, page 1. Reprinted by permission.

warships bombarded anti-Government artillery and missile batteries in mountains southeast of Beirut today.

An American spokesman called it "defensive fire." Maj. Robert Jordan, the United States Marine spokesman, said the naval barrage started after the residence of the United States Ambassador, Robert C. Dillon, in suburban Yarze in the wooded hills overlooking Beirut was exposed to an attack from a multiple rocket launcher.

The residence was not hit, Major Jordan said, but several fires were started in the surrounding woods, where the presidential palace is also situated.

Reporters counted at least 40 rounds fired in roughly a 20-minute period by the two ships, the cruiser Virginia and the destroyer John Rodgers. Afterward, the shelling from the mountains on Beirut appeared to subside. On Monday, according to Western military sources, the two ships fired 368 rounds.

The bombardment followed by several hours the first visit by four to six American Marine peacekeeping troops in Lebanon to the Lebanese Army's front-line position at Suk al Gharb on a ridge overlooking Beirut. The purpose, a marine spokesman said, was to "collect information."

A Problem With Coordinates

According to Western military sources, the Lebanese Army did a poor job Monday of calling in the bombing coordinates for the gunners on the Virginia and the John Rodgers, and as a result the Americans almost hit some villages that were not occupied by anti-Government forces.

The marines were believed to have gone to Suk al Gharb to establish firsthand the proper target coordinates. Reporters who went there today saw American and Lebanese soldiers poring over maps of the area.

Meanwhile, efforts to work out a cease-fire appeared to have foundered.

(Continued on Page A12, Column 1)

You can stop reading at any point beyond the lead paragraph and still have the essence of the story. In print or broadcast, editors have to be tightwads with their time and space. They work in shifts of heartburning flux, where they know the complexion of a newscast or edition only at deadline time. Reporters learn to submit stories that can easily be sheared to fit into whatever space or time allocation is available at the last possible minute.

Broadcast stories are shorter, but the format, called an inverted pyramid because the weight of the piece is heaviest at the top, remains. A broadcast version of this story might read:

> Two American naval vessels blasted anti-government military strongholds in the mountains southeast of Beirut today. The attacks appear to have followed an assault on the residence of US Ambassador Robert C. Dillon. Correspondent Frank Carney has a full report. . . .

COMPONENTS OF A RELEASE

A release is made up of a *lead*, a *body*, and a *conclusion;* in other words, a beginning, middle, and end. At the risk of sounding simplistic, that's all there is to it. It takes practice, but if you bear with it, you'll soon be able to write a release on anything.

The Lead. For now, keep it very simple. Whatever you have to say to the public you'll be able to condense into that simple declarative sentence your English teachers told you about. The best way is to take a few examples.

A lead is your opening three or four sentences, and it should summarize your entire message.

Now, try your hand at a few leads.

1. You're a Certified Public Accountant who can take $2,250 of anyone's money, invest it in an Individual Retirement Account (IRA), protect it from taxation until the owner reaches age sixty-five, and get the government to accept it as a deduction. Your name is Jennifer Barnes, and you live in Menlo Park, California.

2. You're Bob Carter, an executive at Call-Saver, a new telephone company that offers customers a reduction of up to 60 percent on long-distance calls. You want people to know that there's no longer a single telephone company but more than two hundred to choose from, and, of course, you want them to come to you. The combination of government deregulation and competition makes these savings possible.

3. You have a garage full of old car parts—fan belts, transmissions, fenders, radiators, etc.—and you believe you could practically buy a new car from the sale of this junk. So, you're planning a most unusual garage sale three weeks from now. Your name is Les Hanover, and you live at 323 Laurel Street, Manchester, New Hampshire.

4. You're Barbara Parnell of 421 High Street, Chamblee, Georgia. You've just been nominated to run a bake sale to raise money for the local Little League team, and you've been told by your neighbors that they'd like to see some publicity.

5. You're Judy Wright of Rye, New York, and you want the press to know about your new restaurant, Pasta N Things, a unique concept in dining in that your menu is made up of only pasta dishes—spaghetti, lasagne, manicotti, vermicelli, linguine, etc. The address of the restaurant is 101 Woodbine Avenue, Rye, New York. The phone number is (914) 33-PASTA. (Hint: The phone number may or may not be included in the lead, depending on how you decide to

structure it. The same is true with the address, although both will certainly be a part of the release.)

There are no right or wrong formats here, and if your leads don't match the solutions listed below, don't worry. They may be even more appropriate, as long as they're short and to the point.

1. According to Menlo Park accountant Jennifer Barnes, the new IRS laws allow people to save a lot of money on their taxes while availing themselves of a healthy and legal deduction. They can take up to $2,250 of this year's income, invest it in an Individual Retirement Account (IRA), and not have to pay taxes on the money until age sixty-five. Furthermore, the money is deductible from this year's taxes.

2. There used to be only one telephone company, and we had no choice in how much money we spent on long-distance calls. According to Bob Carter, an executive at Call-Saver, however, there are now more than two hundred phone companies to choose from. The result: a reduction of up to 60 percent on long-distance calls. Carter sees this good news as an outgrowth of two factors: deregulation of the telephone industry and advanced technology.

3. A garage sale for weekend automobile enthusiasts will be held on August 11 and 12 at the home of car buff Les Hanover. Hanover, a tinkerer for many years, offers an inventory of carburetors, transmissions, wheels, tires, and other parts from his own garage at 323 Laurel Street in Manchester.

4. Pies, cakes, cupcakes, and brownies provide a delicious backdrop for a bake sale to be held Saturday, May 27, at

421 High Street in Chamblee to raise money for Little League uniforms.

5. Pasta N Things, probably the world's first restaurant to specialize in such treats as cannelloni, linguine, spaghetti, and other gourmet pasta items, opens its doors at 101 Woodbine Avenue in Rye on November 21. Pasta N Things is the brainchild of Judy Wright of Rye, who believes her varied menu will attract pasta fanatics throughout the region.

Those five W's plus H are the building blocks of the lead, but you don't have to religiously get everything in. If you're feeling adventurous, you have other types of leads you can use, as long as you don't overdo it.

The Question Lead
A question at the top of your release can sometimes tantalize an editor into reading further. From the cases we've presented, here are a few examples:

1. Why would the government allow citizens to put $2,250 in taxable income into a bank account, while offering a deduction of that money this year? Menlo Park CPA Jennifer Barnes likes to answer that question.

2. What happened to Ma Bell, and why is she suddenly faced with more than two hundred competing phone companies? According to Call-Saver's Bob Carter, it's a long story that can be shortened to the tune of a 60 percent reduction in long-distance calls.

3. Who wants to buy ten tons of greasy auto parts? Les Hanover of 323 Laurel Street is about to find out.

4. What do cupcakes and croissants have to do with shortstops and catchers? The answer is to be found Saturday, May 27, at the home of Barbara Parnell.

5. Where can a pasta maniac go to indulge in spaghetti, manicotti, vermicelli, and other Mediterranean gourmet delights? They can start with Pasta N Things at 101 Woodbine Avenue in Rye.

You don't always have to answer your questions immediately, but generally it helps.

The Quotation Lead
Sometimes, a quotation from the principal spokesperson of a campaign will offer an alternative that will appeal:

1. "The middle-income wage earner can now enjoy the tax advantages of a big corporation," says Menlo Park accountant Jennifer Barnes.

2. "We used to have only one telephone company," says Bob Carter, a vice president of Call-Saver, "and now we have more than two hundred."

3. "I'm addicted to cars and their parts, and I want to meet lots of other auto maniacs." So, Les Hanover of 323 Laurel Street is having a party.

4. "I hope everyone will eat too many of our delicious pastries," says Mrs. Barbara Parnell of Chamblee. "The calories are for a worthy cause."

5. According to Rye's Judy Wright, "Pasta is good for you and more fun to eat than anything I can think of."

Humorous or Novelty Leads
These are a little more dangerous for the novice publicist, but you should become familiar with novelty or humorous leads. Watch for them and take good notes before trying it yourself. Again, some examples from our hypothetical case histories:

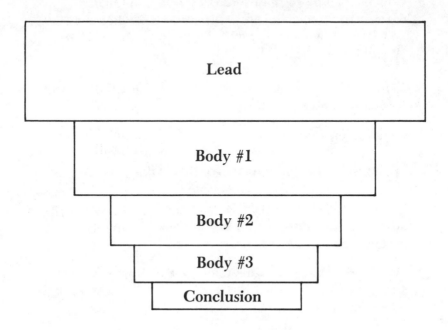

The Inverted Pyramid. The lead paragraph should stress the essence of your campaign in no uncertain terms. Make it simple and direct, highlighting the basic information that you want to convey. Think of it as the only paragraph you have in which to plug yourself. You can then use the following paragraphs to describe the other aspects of your campaign in greater detail.

1. What's way too big and giving away $2,250 this year? According to Menlo Park accountant Jennifer Barnes, it's the federal government.

2. Ma Bell is a widow.

3. Some would say that Les Hanover's garage is full of junk. Others see its contents as something close to erotic.

4. Mrs. Barbara Parnell wants the people of Chamblee to get a little fatter so that a bunch of kids can play ball.

5. Pasta freaks can now come out of the closet.

If there are any rules for novelty leads, they would be to avoid the temptation to be excessively cute and to follow with a concise return to journalistic form.

The Body of Your Release. If you're the compulsive type who wants an absolute blueprint for a release form, here it is:

Lead paragraph

Body paragraph 1

Body paragraph 2

Body paragraph 3 (not always necessary)

Concluding paragraph

Before you actually write the release, it's a good idea to list the facts in descending order of importance, then use words to weld them together. We return again to our five familiar cases.

PRIMARY CAMPAIGN GOAL: To get clients at income tax time

PRIMARY BOOKING ANGLE: $2,250 per year like a gift from Uncle Sam

1. Jennifer Barnes, 71 Tarrytown Road, Menlo Park, California

2. CPA

3. IRAs good for everyone.

4. Tax advantages of big companies available to everyone for the first time.

5. Reason for government programs allowing IRAs—to promote savings, which ultimately helps combat recession.

6. Also helps to combat the effects of an aging Social Security system that's going broke.

7. Office open Monday through Friday, 9:00–5:00.

PRIMARY CAMPAIGN GOAL: To increase Call-Saver share in growing long-distance telephone market

PRIMARY BOOKING ANGLE: Reduced cost of long-distance calls

1. Robert W. Carter, vice president, consumer relations, Call-Saver Inc., 153 Cedar Park Lane, Waco, Texas

2. Antitrust legislation has forced the breakup of AT&T, opening the telephone field to competitors for the very first time.

3. Technology enables companies to charge up to 60 percent less for calls.

4. Call-Saver was recently set up to serve the growing need for economical long-distance calls.

5. The company is made up of more than five hundred communications professionals with previous telephone company experience.

6. Call-Saver uses the most modern equipment.

7. Call-Saver differs from other "new" telephone companies in two ways: It charges less and the reception quality of the calls is superior.

8. Call-Saver offers its customers a free telephone.

PRIMARY CAMPAIGN GOAL: To sell a garageful of car parts

PRIMARY BOOKING ANGLE: A garage sale for car buffs

1. Every kind of car part imaginable.

2. Lester Hanover knows he can build a complete car from the parts in his garage. He's done it before.

3. He's been accumulating parts since he moved into the house in 1955.

4. A tinkerer all his life, Hanover hopes the sale will introduce him to other car buffs.

PRIMARY CAMPAIGN GOAL: To raise money for baseball uniforms through a bake sale

PRIMARY BOOKING ANGLE: Tempt a little weight for the good of the kids

1. Sale to feature homemade cakes, cupcakes, brownies, etc.

2. Sale to occur Saturday, November 23, between 10:00 A.M. and 4:00 P.M. at 421 High Street.

3. Rain date is Sunday, November 24.

PRIMARY CAMPAIGN GOAL: To attract customers to Pasta N Things

PRIMARY BOOKING ANGLE: The novelty of a restaurant serving only pasta dishes

1. A restaurant serving only pasta dishes.

2. Believed to be the world's only restaurant of its kind.

3. More than 35 gourmet pasta specialties to choose from.

4. Specialties include Manicotti Supreme, eighteen spaghetti dishes, the Cannelloni Adventure, Vermicelli Napoli, Lasagne Fantasy, and Linguine Divine. A special low-calorie section of the menu.

5. Opens on December 11.

The Conclusion. A release's final paragraph or *conclusion* might be a concise summation of your primary booking angle, a final opportunity to reiterate booking contact information, or a parcel of additional information that is relevant but not important enough to have been included earlier. The only rule for conclusions is that they differ from all other paragraphs because of a sense of finality. Review the samples on pages 38–43, practice with our hypothetical case histories, and try your hand at it.

HOMEWORK

Before you move ahead to the next chapter, where you'll be putting your press release together, practice assembling inverted-pyramid formats and final draft releases for each of the five examples provided.

THE SHORT BIO

A biography on a release is optional, but many current handouts do contain them. For our purposes here, a biography is a brief description of credentials and other key public components of a person's life. Most important, it is a summary of one's life *as it applies to the primary booking angle of the campaign*. If you're trying to sell yourself as an adult long out of school, your high school dramatic achievement award isn't going to pack them in the aisles.

> Dr. Doreen Carney has been practicing pediatrics in Waltham for more than twenty-five years. A 1952 graduate of Bishop Stang high school, Dr. Carney attended Stonehill College and Boston University School of Medicine. She has published more than twenty-five articles in professional journals and received the 1973 Blum Award for outstanding contributions to the well-being of Waltham. She currently resides and practices at 4 Crestview Road with her husband, Professor Brian Wallin of M.I.T., and her daughter, Carolyn, a student at Waltham High.

THE FORMAT OF A RELEASE

Whether it appears on an $8\frac{1}{2}" \times 11"$ sheet of paper, the standard size of a typing sheet, or the legal-sized $8\frac{1}{2}" \times 14"$, a release should always be neat and in accordance with a traditional format. While there are several ways to do it, and no one will give you a failing grade if you deviate a little, we offer the following specifications for a release.

The Release Date. You can either specify that you want your publicity to run on a given date by saying, "FOR RELEASE JANUARY 12, 1985," or use the time-honored "FOR IMMEDIATE RELEASE." For your purposes, the latter is probably more practical; formal release dates are still in use with the automotive industry, the various government agencies, and in a variety of other settings, but even there they are ignored; the press figures, rightly so, that anything sent to them is fair game. They, too, are in a highly competitive business, in which success often depends upon not being polite.

The release date should go at the top left corner of your release, five spaces below either the letterhead, if you're using one, or the upper edge of the paper. Either capitalize the first letter of each of the three words or put the whole thing in upper case.

The Contact. The simple word *contact*, as in

Contact Kathleeen Brown (312) 877-4848, Ext. 321

should appear three spaces below the "FOR IMMEDIATE RELEASE" heading. You should feel free to expand the phraseology to "For Further Information Contact _____" if you prefer. Sometimes the contact information appears at the bottom of the page; place it anywhere you like outside the main body of the release, but putting it at the top guarantees some attention to this vital component of your release.

The Headline. The headline is next, and it should appear about three spaces above the lead paragraph. It isn't necessary to use all caps, but it's a good idea to separate it in some way—italics, different typeface, boldface, etc.—from the rest of your copy. The headline says something about what you're selling and should be reworked many times before a decision is made. Remember that it's one of life's few opportunities to get away with not using a complete sentence. Read the newspaper carefully to observe the fine art of headline writing before trying it yourself. The headline should be centered.

Paragraphs. Don't waste a lot of time trying to decide whether to indent three spaces or to run flush with the margin and skip a line between paragraphs. You're right either way.

Margins. Whatever looks good will suffice as a margin so long as you're consistent. You can't go wrong with a "15" setting on the left and "85" on the right. Avoid the temptation to skid past your right margin to squeeze in a long word.

The Bottom of a Page. Be careful not to type beyond three spaces from the bottom of your page.

Both Sides Versus Two Sheets. Our position is to use a second sheet instead of printing on both sides of a page, but it's far from a universally accepted tenet of release writing. Typing on both sides of a legal sheet means that the whole release is in the editor's hands at once. But using two sheets is usually neater.

Legal-Size Paper Versus Standard. The fewer pages the better. It's better to have a single-page release on a legal-sized sheet than a page and a half on two standard sheets. But there's nothing wrong with either format.

Single Versus Double Spacing. No debate here. Your main body should be double-spaced with single spacing included if you want to set something off. Quoting a paragraph from a medical journal is an example of using a single spacing within a double-spaced release.

Length of a Release. Try to confine your release to two pages.

Ending It. An ancient press tradition is to use "-30-" as the final indicator of a story. This is a signal between editors and printers that is sometimes used to conclude releases. "-30-" is optional, as is the practice of triple asterisks (***) as an indicator. Your final sentence is certainly enough by itself.

Reproduction. Everyone seems to have an in-law or uncle with an office where a little after-hours copying or mimeographing won't hurt anyone. Tell your uncle thanks but no thanks and go to a printer.

Offset is a photographic reproduction printing process that requires that a release be "camera ready," meaning typed on a professional machine and free of error. It is considerably cheaper than *typesetting* a release, or reproducing your copy as print, but it isn't quite so good-looking.

Either way, printing is one of the big bargains of a publicity campaign, eliminating such problems as faded type, grittiness due to a copying machine that needs cleaning, and other taints of amateurism. A printer can also provide sound advice on weight of paper, texture, colors, and other options.

Paper Stock and Colors. Black-on-white is still probably your best bet for a release, although you are by no means restricted to it. If your topic is fun, have a little fun with beige stock, or any color you choose. Don't use a flimsy paper. Go to a stationery store where paper is sold by the ream and feel the texture of the various options before making the choice.

The Postcard Release. The U.S. Postal Service doesn't object if you use a postcard format to convey your message to the press. Your printer will have up-to-date information on the sizes the Postal Service will allow through the mail. Since regulations change periodically, it's also a good idea to check with your local post office. If you have something that can be said in a few lines, the postcard release offers one advantage that is unbeatable: It doesn't have to be opened and is thus more likely to be read.

If you've practiced enough with our case histories and feel you're now ready to do your own release, move ahead to the next chapter. If you still feel a little rough around the edges with release writing, work at it a little longer before moving on.

FOR IMMEDIATE RELEASE

Contact: Jennifer Barnes
(415) 623-0318

NEW TAX LAWS SAVE MILLIONS
FOR AMERICAN CONSUMERS

According to Menlo Park accountant Jennifer Barnes, people can save a lot more of their pre-tax income this year. They can take $2,250.00 of their annual income, invest it in an Individual Retirement Account (IRA), and not have to pay taxes on it until they reach age sixty-five, when they are likely to be in a lower tax bracket. The best news is that the money is deductible from this year's taxes.

"The government is equalizing the taxation process by allowing anyone to invest in an IRA," says Ms. Barnes, who specializes in legitimate tax loopholes for middle-income wage earners. "For the first time in our nation's history people of limited means can enjoy the same tax benefits as a major corporation," she says.

Ms. Barnes believes the reasoning behind the new tax incentive plans is twofold: to strengthen the economy through savings, and to combat the erosion of a Social Security System that is itself aging and will eventually be ill-equipped to offer people very much financial comfort during their later years.

A problem that the thirty-two-year-old CPA faces daily is either disbelief on the part of her clients, who are accustomed to thinking of legitimate tax avoidance as illegal, or a tendency to procrastinate in financial planning. Because she believes that an investment portfolio is as essential to a household as insurance policies, real estate, and other long-range systems, Ms. Barnes offers a free educational consultation to anyone earning less than $75,000 annually. Her office at 71 Tarrytown Road in Menlo Park is open between nine and five, Monday through Friday. Her phone number is 623-0318.

—30—

FOR IMMEDIATE RELEASE

Contact: Terry Ball
       (514) 564-4766

TELEPHONE EXECUTIVE URGES CONSUMERS TO
SHOP CAREFULLY FOR PHONE CALLS

"We used to have only one telephone company," says Bob
Carter, Vice President of Operations at Call-Saver, "and now
we have more than two hundred." Call-Saver of Waco, Texas,
is the newest of the freshly minted phone companies that have
emerged in the wake of new antitrust legislation that forced
the breakup of AT&T and opened the field to competition for
the first time.

Call-Saver was established to serve the growing demand for
long-distance calls, which have, thanks to the forces of free
market competition and government deregulation, been
reduced in cost by as much as 60 percent. One of Carter's
principal aims is to convince people that such saving is
available. A stumbling block is that people often tell him that
his service is "too good to be true."

"People are naturally suspicious of anything that goes
against that which they've seen all their lives. Since the
nineteenth century, phones have been a virtual monopoly in
this country, but that's all history now," Mr. Carter says.

Call-Saver is comprised of more than five hundred
communications professionals with prior telephone company
experience. The company utilizes the most modern technology
available and plans to continue doing so.

But how is Call-Saver different from other phone
companies? According to Carter, the answer to that question is
uncomplicated. Call-Saver is superior in two ways: It charges
less per call, and the reception quality of its transmitting
system is superior. Call-Saver also offers its customers a free
telephone manufactured to the highest technical standards.

Information on the new telephone technology is available without obligation at Call-Saver's toll-free number, 1-800-555-4921, or by writing to Call-Saver Inc., 153 Cedar Park Lane, Waco, TX 98765.

–30–

FOR IMMEDIATE RELEASE

Contact: Lester Hanover
         (603) 622-2232

AUTO BUFF PLANS GARAGE SALE
FOR OTHER AUTO BUFFS

Who wants to buy ten tons of greasy auto parts? Les Hanover of 323 Laurel Street in Manchester is about to find out. Hanover, a lifetime weekend automobile tinkerer, has scheduled a garage sale for auto enthusiasts to be held in his garage on August 11 and 12 between 10:00 A.M. and 6:00 P.M., rain or shine.

Hanover claims there are enough carburetors, transmissions, body parts, engine components, tires, batteries, and wheels in his garage to build a complete automobile. In fact, Hanover has built three of them since 1955. If the sale matches Mr. Hanover's expectations, he plans to turn it into an annual event. Questions on inventory may be directed to Mr. Hanover any day after 6:00 P.M. by calling 622-2232.

–30–

FOR IMMEDIATE RELEASE

Contact: Barbara Parnell
       (404) 321-2121

BAKE SALE TO BE HELD FOR CHAMBLEE

LITTLE LEAGUE

"I hope everyone will eat too many of our delicious
pastries," says Mrs. Barbara Parnell of Chamblee. "The
calories are for a worthy cause."

The worthy cause is Chamblee's Perry Foster Knights of
Columbus Little League team, named for the legendary coach
of Chamblee High who retired last year after thirty years and
eleven state baseball championships. The new team needs
$480 to outfit the twenty-two major leaguers of tomorrow, and
Mrs. Parnell will hold a bake sale Saturday, November 23,
between 10:00 A.M. and 4:00 P.M. at her home, located at 421
High Street in Chamblee. Pies, cakes, croissants, doughnuts,
brownies, and other treats will be available. Sunday,
November 24, will be the event's rain date. Donations of
pastry or cash for the uniforms can be arranged by calling
Mrs. Parnell at 321-2121.

–30–

FOR IMMEDIATE RELEASE

Contact: Judy Wright
      (914) 337-2782

GOURMET PASTA RESTAURANT TO OPEN IN RYE

Pasta N Things, probably the world's first restaurant to specialize in such treats as cannelloni, linguine, spaghetti, and other gourmet pasta items, opens its doors at 101 Woodbine Avenue in Rye on December 11. Pasta N Things is the brainchild of Rye's Judy Wright, who believes her varied menu will attract pasta fanatics throughout the region.

"Pasta is a way of life for those of us who are hooked on it," she says. "And it's actually very good for you, a very healthful food." Ms. Wright disdains the notion that pasta is a threat to a thin waistline. Most of the calories associated with pasta are actually a function of the sauce. With careful preparation and discretionary use of oil, she has developed a "calorie counter" portion of the menu where no entree contains more than 500 calories.

The thirty-five-year-old rookie restaurateur points with pride to her thirty-five gourmet pasta specialties, which include Manicotti Supreme, eighteen variations of spaghetti offerings, the Cannelloni Adventure, Vermicelli Napoli, Lasagne Fantasy, and Linguine Divine. Pasta N Things will be open daily for lunch and dinner and plans to honor all major credit cards.

–30–

Your Press Kit

Having done some release isometrics on hypothetical examples, you're ready to try writing yourself up. For some, this is easy. Others find it so excruciating that they call in a friend for a rewrite or editing job, or to do the entire release. All of those measures are permissible, of course, but our recommendation is to do a couple of drafts yourself first. Some guidelines:

- Reexamine your primary campaign goal and booking angle to be sure that each is defined and refined.

- Check to be sure that the facts in your campaign are all there and that they're arranged in an inverted-pyramid style (descending order of importance).

- If you're stuck on form, remember the skeletal basis for any release: Lead + Paragraph + Paragraph + Conclusion. (Remember too that being too long can be a problem but that a release can almost never be too short.)

- If you feel you still need practice and have worked over the five examples in Chapter 5 *ad nauseam*, choose your own examples and work on them. This part of the campaign seems to take a long time, but soon you'll be rolling quite rapidly.

- Review the five Ws plus H as they apply to your project.

- Without interrupting yourself, write your whole release in a first draft. Don't worry yet about grammar, phrasing, spelling, punctuation, or overall mood of the release. Worry about doing it all the way through without stopping.

- Now doctor up your work with punctuation, synonyms, and other spices of the language. You may want to read it aloud or have someone read it to you.

- Do a few more drafts, until you're reasonably sure that it's smooth. Remember, don't be intimidated.

- Give yourself about ten headline options after you've concluded the main body. Consult a newspaper to see how a story comparable to your own is headlined.

- Resolve to be clear and accurate but to finish this job rapidly. There's still a lot more to do.

THE PRESS KIT

A press kit is a packet of information that offers editors, producers, and interviewers all they need to know about you. The release is the centerpiece of a kit but there are other components that complete the packaged version of your campaign.

Not everyone agrees that a press kit is necessary to a publicity effort. If you're out to promote a single local event, a postcard release will more than suffice. But most campaigns *will* benefit from a kit that contains a few standard publicity fixtures that you should plan on using:

NEWS

Barbara J. Hendra Associates, Inc. • Empire State Building • Suite 1101 • 350 Fifth Avenue • New York, NY 10118 • 212/947-9898

VICTOR SYRMIS
President, Chocolate Photos

VICTOR SYRMIS, the entrepreneurial wiz behind the new company Chocolate
Photos, a New York-based firm that creates cameos in chocolate, has his roots
not in the confectionary trade, as one might think, but in the medical field.

"I think that everybody has fascinating ideas, but some people just can't
get them out into the world," says the doctor, "And everyone has the entrepreneurial
spirit."

Syrmis certainly has it. Two years ago, Syrmis was searching Madison Avenue
for a unique gift for his wife when he came upon a store specializing in computerized
head sculptures of customers. He jokingly asked if a head could be done in chocolate,
but he soon turned the joke into an exciting business venture.

After much research, Syrmis, working with two artists, developed the process
in which a line drawing made from a photograph is turned into a foil mold, into
which either dark or milk chocolate is poured. Chocolate Photos was born, with
Critchley's Candies, Bergen County, New Jersey, as the manufacturer.

Syrmis, 39, was born in Ayr in northern Australia. After graduating from
medical school in Melbourne in 1967, he spent six months in New Guinea practicing
medicine. A year later, he moved to Hamilton, Canada, a town just outside Toronto.

Chocolate Photos .

- more -

The Biography. It can be a paragraph or two at the end of a release
or, as pictured here, a separate write-up.

The Folder. Any stationery store will offer many folders, and you should probably opt for a nonflamboyant, standard (8½″ × 11½″) in white, gray, blue, or black.

The Long Bio. The "long bio" is a one- or two-page biography of your experience. If the information on your release is sufficient, or if you have chosen a "short bio," leave this element out. If you need a page or two to cover your credentials, set it off as a separate component of the press kit. Here is a checklist for the long bio:

- ☐ Schools attended, with years of graduation

- ☐ Education beyond local schools

- ☐ Year married

- ☐ Spouse's name and local schools attended

- ☐ Children

- ☐ Current occupation

- ☐ Prior positions if applicable

- ☐ Professional credentials that apply to campaign

- ☐ Local awards and other listings of civic participation

If you are a physician, an academic, or a member of a profession where a curriculm vitae might be in order, submit one, but only if the information would be of real interest to those considering you for an interview. If you are seeking publicity on a professional level, such as in journals, a vitae is more than a fine idea. If you're going to appear with the host of an afternoon movie on the local UHF, hide your laurels under the guise of being a "regular guy," even if you're a woman! Impressive

A *Product Press Kit*. Depending on the product, a kit such as this one will contain anywhere from three to ten pieces of informational material. See pages 66-67 for the individual components.

The Outside Folder

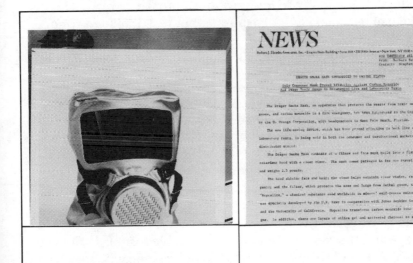

An Open Kit

Press kit courtesy of Barbara J. Hendra Associates, Inc.

professional credentials often inspire fear in interviewers.

A resume follows the same course. If there's an application to your primary campaign goal, use it; if there's not a lot in it that is pertinent to your sales pitch, shelve it.

The Cover Letter. The cover letter is a pitch between you and the media source. You're doing the selling. You're telling why you want to be interviewed and, more to the point, why you should be interviewed.

In its ideal form, a pitch letter should be typed on a single page, slanted to a particular individual, and written without a lot of hype. The usual practice is to draft a three-paragraph letter, adding the name of the addressee and a few specifics that counteract the form-letter tone that is despised in every corner of broadcast and print.

In many cases it helps for the cover letter and the follow-up phone call to be from someone other than you. You might want to adapt a pseudonym for pitching yourself, or perhaps a friend can be persuaded, blackmailed, or hired to do the phone work. But if you feel that you want to represent yourself, you won't be alone, and no one will laugh at you for doing so. Develop a thick skin in either case.

The Question and Answer (Q&A). Only a few years ago, editors and producers were apt to growl menacingly at the notion that a public relations source might be so audacious as to suggest questions. Today, they'll say, "So, where are the sample questions?" Said questions are submitted in two ways: the Q&A that serves as an actual interview, or a list of ten or fifteen questions without answers.

The Q&A usually is set up with the questions in bold type or all caps and the answers in italics. A suitable form is both sides of an 8½″ × 14″ sheet of paper, although no one will place you under arrest if you use 8½″ × 11″. Whether you use two sides of a single sheet or a separate sheet for each side, four pages should be enough. Edit carefully so as to avoid every little clearing of throat, conversational ramble, or other aspect of speech that might not fit into a printed format.

Questions Without Answers. To give the kit credibility, be tough and straight. The following are good examples of questions that aren't adoring and self-serving. If you have difficulty thinking up questions about your project, use the following general questions as guidelines:

QUESTIONS FOR ____ ____ ON _____

1. What is a _____?

2. Why do we need it?

3. What does your _____ do that other _____s don't?

4. Why did you develop _____?

5. _____ _____, writing in _____ _____, says that _____ s are a waste of time. Can you defend developing one yourself?

6. What are the special marketing and distribution problems of _____?

7. Who is most likely to benefit from your _____?

8. Who are the most enthusiastic boosters of your _____?

9. _____ _____, writing in the *Journal of* _____, says that _____s such as yours are the wave of the future and by 1990, _____ out of every four Americans will have one. Are you that optimistic yourself?

10. Your biography says that you attended _____ College. Did the inspiration for the _____ come from your days there?

11. How has this city changed since you were in school?

12. Are there any dangers to _____ that we should know about?

13. Your resume says that in addition to _____ you have a very interesting hobby. Would you discuss it with us?

14. Your wife (husband) is also from _____. Why did you decide to make your home in this community?

15. What's ahead for you?

Notice that questions 5 and 9 are reverses of the same theme. If there is a published source in opposition to what you are doing or saying and you feel you can strongly defend your project, by all means include it in the question.

The Photo. Snapshots are out in press kits, but a black-and-white, 8″ × 10″ or 5″ × 7″ photograph is a must. These pictures should be photographed with a 35mm camera, and if you have any doubt about the quality, get a friend or hire a professional. Never scrimp on photos; like printing, they are generally available economically. If you know something about photography and have access to a good 35mm, all the better. If not, shop around.

The next photographic decision is a head-and-shoulders portrait versus an action shot of you at work. If an action shot best reveals what you're selling with your primary campaign goal, get one. Otherwise, the traditional "yearbook" shot is perfectly acceptable.

The Photo Session. If it is the only component of your press kit published, a picture is worth a lot more than a thousand words. If your primary booking angle is the promotion of a restaurant, a tool, a product, or some other object, you'll need a photograph of it in the kit. Because your photo is so important, you should visit with several professional photographers for an estimate of both the cost of a photo session and the cost of reproducing the number of pictures you think you'll need for the campaign. The following tips should help you make photo decisions:

1. Before your session with a photographer, decide how you want to look. For some, a head and shoulders shot is wonderful. Others are better off in action at work.

2. Ask the photographer to help you choose your best side. Don't be bashful about having shots taken from eight or more different angles and poses. When the sessions are over, you will be shown either proofs or contact sheets. Proofs are preliminary photographs printed on special paper; sooner or later, they'll fade. They exist only to show what an enlarged print of your photograph will look like. Contact sheets are the reproduction of a whole strip of shots on a single sheet of photographic paper. Usually, you examine the shots under a magnifying glass.

3. If the photographer takes the pictures at your home or place of business, be sure that there are no eye-catching distractions behind you. A sailboat, for example, might be a nice possession to show your friends, but it could distract from you in a publicity shot.

4. If you're unhappy with the lighting or any other aspect of how you look, reshoot.

Promotional Insert

Photograph

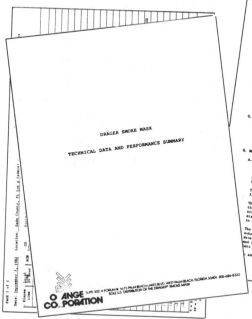

Technical Data

Questions and Answers

Product Test Results

Supplementary Releases

5. A one- or two-line caption that describes the photograph
   should be typed camera-ready and given to the
   photographer for printing. For example, "Colonel John
   Zyla with 'Cookie,' his favorite palomino. Zyla breeds and
   sells palominos at his Grab Bag Ranch in Merrimack, New
   Hampshire."

GRAPHICS

Your printer can direct you toward many intriguing logos,
type styles, and other graphics that will embellish your press
kit. Check prices very carefully, and avoid a lot of fancy gloss
that will strike the media person as too slick. On the other
hand, don't attempt any home-brew calligraphy here. When
in doubt about graphics, skip them.

Here, then is a recipe for your press kit:

1 2-page release, offset or typeset (If you can say it all in one
page, all the better.)

1 or 2 photographs (5" × 7" is probably easier to work with
than 8" × 10", and the press is used to photographs of this
dimension.)

1 Q&A list of questions

1 cover letter, no more than a single page

1 sturdy folder

7

The Campaign Strategy

We're now at the starting gate, the point where you make decisions on what type of exposure you wish to use for yourself. Targeting your publicity is equivalent to preparing a battle plan or a political strategy and should be approached with comparable attention to detail.

There are really only three media strategies—local, regional, and national, with the latter being either a finale to the campaign or a goal for future efforts. Chapter 25 will deal extensively with national exposure. For now, plan on sticking to the grass roots. That's where even the most illustrious generally start.

Set up a campaign room or corner with a map on constant display. This might sound a little prescribed, even pretentious, but as you progress, you're guaranteed to see the value of having a place to go every time you wish to work on the campaign.

From this point, you should spend a segment of every working day on the campaign. It can't move on a piecemeal basis, for all effectiveness in publicity is based on momentum. Scan the map for its geographical possibilities, bearing in mind that you're looking to sell something to potential customers. Where are these consumers of your brainstorm likely to be? Perhaps

most of them are twenty miles from your front door; perhaps
they're all over the world.

Start with a city or town in your region that is similar in
makeup to your home base, on the assumption that it's better
to take an act to New Haven before trying Broadway. Draw a
circle around that town and label it with a "1," meaning that
it's the first media center you wish to target. Follow a similar
procedure for four more towns in your region, bearing in mind
that you're better off working away from a big city at
first.

If you live in a city, go toward the suburbs for your first appearances. Since our publicity blueprint starts with weekly
newspapers and public-affairs radio programs, there is no need
to wait very long to target large population centers; but for
openers, the congenial tone of small markets will be more conducive to building confidence. That's what it's all about
now.

In your thinking, as in the standard dictum of mediaspeak,
cities and towns will now become "markets." All population
centers are ranked by demographers; New York is #1, Los Angeles is #2, and Flagstaff is #208. Your own first five markets
should be chosen on the basis of their access to you and whether
your primary campaign goal has any bearing on the needs of
the population.

Once you've made these five choices, it's time to find out
what media outlets are available to you. The local telephone
directory is a good start, but you'll need more advanced reference material from your public library. In the extremely rare
instances in which a library can't help, there is often a local advertising agency or public-relations firm (in small markets they
tend to be one and the same) where you can take notes. See
Chapter 8 for all the specifics, and Chapter 27 for a list of
available reference materials.

RADIO

The twenty-four-hour talk stations in larger cities are your "A" targets and probably should not be approached yet. Your "B" stations are local live talk shows in medium-sized cities (roughly, 100,000–300,000 in metro population) and the "C" programs, your start in broadcasting, are the public-affairs programs you logged in Chapter 2.

The source material will list program directors and public-affairs directors, which can so often make it all confusing. Sometimes, the news director is also the public-affairs director. As a rule of thumb, plan to write to the radio program director in small and medium markets and the public-affairs director in large cities.

Type out the names and addresses of your radio targets (call the station and ask for the program director's name if there's any doubt), making sure that in your best judgment you've listed them in "A," "B," and "C" order. Now you have a master radio mailing list. (Make sure you maintain a file copy of your master mailing list, because you may wish to use it beyond this campaign.) Assemble your press kits, stuff them in manila envelopes or jiffy bags, type the addresses on labels, and stack them in a corner. You're not ready to mail them just yet.

TELEVISION

You probably have spent more time with TV during the last twenty or thirty years than you have with any spouse, teacher, lover, friend, or parent. It's more of an appendage than a medium. Thus, you might be a little dazzled by the notion of moving from your living room to the inside of the tube, but there's nothing to worry about. You're going on television soon, and it will be fun as long as you don't get too ambitious.

For the purpose of compiling your strategy, we'll skip a lot of intermediate points in favor of two broad categories.

Television "A" is a daily talk show or combination news and talk show while a "B" is a weekly public-affairs interview program. If you haven't kept a log of these local programs, take the chute back to Chapter 2 and do so now, for it is important that you concentrate only on the "B" category for the moment. Now compile a master list of "B" programs; you'll probably have to do some calling to find out the names of the producers. Once more, put the names on labels, put the kits inside the jiffy bags and the labels on the outside, and put the bags to one side. Again, make sure that you maintain a file copy of the mailing list.

CABLE

Generally all public-access cable programs are funneled through the program manager of a system, and the host you see on screen functions as the producer. Repeat the process for cable, bearing in mind that you're looking for local-access shows rather than network offerings. It's often difficult to separate them in the tangled web of cable-viewing options. If you're having difficulty here, simply call the cable system, ask for the programming department, announce that you're compiling a list of local talk shows, and ask if they can help by listing some of their more enduring programs.

NEWSPAPERS

File the weekly newspapers as "B"s and the dailies as "A"s, look up the editors' names, and make your lists, again stuffing the envelopes and separating carefully. The newspaper scenario is less rigid than broadcasting, where it's virtually imperative that you start small. Our strongest advice is to read your target publications and get to know something about who does what and on what page. If possible, do the weeklies first. This sometimes presents a problem because there are extreme differences among weeklies; sometimes they're simply not professional enough to be worth your time. Make your best judgment, but stay out of big-city newsrooms until you've had some practice with reporters.

THE BOOKING SEQUENCE

There are no hard-and-fast rules now. It's all up to you. Our recommended sequence of building blocks is as follows:

Radio B—Weekly public-affairs shows

Newspaper B (including small magazines)—Weekly newspapers

Cable—Public-access programs

Television B—Local public-affairs programs in any market

Radio A—Live talk shows in any size market

Newspaper A—Daily newspaper profiles

Television A—Daily talk shows in any market

You may wish to read the following chapters on interview preparation now, or you might prefer to teethe a little on the "B" media first. Our position is that the best preparation for radio is public-affairs interviews in small markets, the best preparation for television is local cable, and the weekly newspapers are a wonderful print-interview lab. If you're tired of stuffing envelopes, get your feet wet here. Just stay away from the "A"s for now. Mail your "B" press kits, make your follow-up calls, and go on the air.

8

Your First Interviews

Public-affairs and cable talk shows are easy to book. Whether you're in a one-street prairie town a thousand miles from the nearest Woolworth's or in midtown Manhattan, the procedure rarely varies. You send a "B" press kit, follow it up with a call, and set a date for the interview.

You may discover, to your This-Is-Easier-Than-I-Thought joy, that your mailing results in the station calling you. If it happens, enjoy it. This is the only phase of the campaign where such an event is likely to occur. In most cases, your follow-up call is awaited. Don't be surprised if it is not returned. In the media scheme of things, ordinary rules of social conduct don't always apply. The producer who would never even consider not calling back in other situations routinely ignores mounting messages in favor of getting the pressing work at hand behind her or him. Editors and producers are on a constant deadline, which sometimes takes precedence over the courtesy of returning telephone calls. Don't take it personally.

Persistence, then, is one of your first and most important lessons in telephone contact work. When you do get your contact on the phone, don't be surprised if she or he sounds rushed. Get used to that as well and don't let it throw you. Just get to the point quickly and with confidence.

For a little perspective on whom you'll be talking to through the campaign, here's a quick glossary of media titles and what you might expect from those holding them:

Producer.   This is one of the most common titles in the talk field; it can mean anything from a powerful person around the station to a twerp who runs for coffee. In most local settings, read "producer" as the person responsible for booking the guests on a talk show.

Associate Producer.   In major market settings (big cities), there may be two or three associate producers who specialize in the booking of specific guest categories such as entertainers, authors, local community groups, antiques specialists, or cooking segments. For the most part, an associate producer takes your calls and decides if he or she wants to sponsor your idea and book it on the show.

Talent Coordinator.   On large network shows, talent coordinators are responsible for pre-interviewing guests: having a conversation with a potential guest to determine that person's suitability for a particular program. In medium markets, the title is often applied to a freshman booker, while in smaller towns, the talent coordinator fetches coffee and parks your car.

News Director.   There's a reason beyond ego why anyone with this title takes himself seriously. In any setting, the news director has to be the representative of fair journalism and First Amendment rights, a difficult task in a one-horse station where sponsors, tinhorn politicians, and other two-bit power brokers think they can control what goes out over the air. In small radio stations, the news director is the whole department. In large television stations, the title implies a Lou Grant type who commands a fleet of vans, helicopters, remote satellite units, and other state-of-the-art reporting implements. Regardless of the setup, any time you end up with a "news" person, stay as far away from hype as you can.

News Producer. You'll meet them when you're appearing on combination news and talk shows. The news producer is a line foreman who has to keep rearranging the priorities of a broadcast until (and even after) the shows goes on the air.

Talent. The general term applying to people who go on the air, and one of the reasons for an institutionalized ego sense among these folks. Ted Baxter was no figment of some writer's imagination. You'll meet him often.

Engineer. The technical person responsible for maintaining logs and equipment to FCC specifications. Engineers rarely have engineering degrees but they are often licensed with a General Radiotelephone Certificate from the FCC, a document awarded only on completion of rigorous technical examinations. You won't be writing to engineers, but make friends with them when you can. They tend to have the attention of everyone in a station.

Executive Producer. Read that one as boss of the talk show and act accordingly.

Program Director. In small and medium markets, this person is the head disc jockey. In large cities, the job signifies the executive responsible for everything that goes on the air. Television is apt to tag the slot "program manager."

Editor. The person in charge of reporters, generally in television and newspapers only. In radio, the title usually exists in large stations only.

Reporter. The person a newspaper, television station, or magazine assigns to interview and write about you. They tend to shun overt flattery but, like anyone else, are responsive if you show a sincere interest in them. Always play it straight with reporters. Like police officers, they have well-developed ESP and will handle your case in a manner dictated by their professional instincts.

Investigative Reporter. A muckraker who is committed to uncovering the dark side of a story. You'll not meet them in the normal course of a campaign, but if you are involved with a more probing reporter, and you really do have something you prefer to omit, see Chapter 18.

Assignment Editor. The person who chooses or fails to choose a reporter to interview you.

If your "B" material is in one place, or perhaps already mailed, and you choose the "get wet" option of a public-affairs interview, make your follow-up calls (or get some help in doing so) and go on the air. If you would prefer to wait, read through Chapter 17 before moving on.

9
Booking

After the public-affairs shows and weekly newspapers, there is an art to booking an interview. Booking is persuading a media source to schedule an interview. Even the most experienced PR professionals will often admit that they developed sloppy booking habits early in their careers and that such untidiness, once imprinted, presents problems later. Bad booking habits are sirens that whisper seductive aphorisms about saving time, skipping steps, achieving the same results with half the work.

A problem is that "mouth booking," the cold solicitation of a media source without prior correspondence, sometimes works very well. But if you're planning a campaign that will take you to networks, through large cities, or to print publications with sizable circulations, there is a structure that costs extra time initially but saves many hours once the momentum of a campaign takes over.

Whether you're going for a guest shot on *Aunt Kay's Kitchen*, or planning to nail an industrial polluter on *Sixty Minutes*, the most efficient booking procedure requires only five steps.

DEVELOPMENT OF A MAILING LIST PRIOR TO THE CAMPAIGN

Even though you've been through the reference books, people change their jobs very often. It's a good idea to make a preliminary check of your more important sources. For example:

"Good afternoon, WFEA."

"I have some correspondence for Mr. Ray Fournier. Is he still news director?"

"I'm sorry, Mr. Fournier is no longer with us. Mr. Dave Peretz is now news director."

"Thank you."

A little call like that can make a big difference in whether or not a station makes a booking. Press people often discard correspondence for their predecessors but open mail addressed to them. Even if you're mailing a kit, the pitch letter should be in its own envelope with the addressee's name in plain sight. Some shrewd publicists even write the contact name in their own penmanship, figuring (often correctly) that such a personal touch will be more likely to get attention.

THE PRE-CALL

"Dave Peretz."

"Mr. Peretz, my name is Bob Carter, and I'm a vice president of Call-Saver. I'm sending along some consumer information on how to save up to 60 percent on long-distance calls. I'm hoping you'll take a look and perhaps consider an interview."

"Sounds interesting, Mr. Carr . . ."

"Carter, actually."

"Sorry, I'm terrible at names. Anyway, it sounds interesting but a little commercial for us."

"I know. That's why I'm focusing on general issues. Naturally, I'm hoping to get my company name in, but the emphasis is on saving money in general."

"I'll take a look and get back to you."

He'll take a look. That's the whole purpose of the pre-call. It is nothing more than a brief introduction and a solicitation to watch for something in the mail. The pre-call saves a lot of time, because the source sometimes refers you immediately to a more specialized colleague who is more likely to do the interview. In other cases, you'll be stopped right in the middle of a sentence and politely informed that there is no way at all that this person is able or willing to do the interview. At the very least, the contact is alerted to a specific piece of mail. Professional publicists who have to work on the telephone daily sometimes either skip the pre-call or use it as a booking pitch because of a familiarity with the contact. Since you are working out for the first time, the pre-call is highly recommended.

THE MAILING

If you live in a small community, you might want to take a ride and drop your press kits off in a single afternoon. Otherwise, use first-class mail and padded envelopes. The U.S. Postal Service is anything but dainty. The beautiful press kits you've assembled will arrive looking like last November's turkey if you skimp here. Gimmicky deliveries by costumed messengers or the use of expensive express-mail services are unnecessary.

THE FOLLOW-UP CALL

Don't wait for anyone to call you. Within five days of your material's arrival, you should be on the phone with a well-planned pitch no longer than thirty seconds in duration. If this sounds like a difficult pursuit, don't feel like a failure. Most

people talk too long, become tongue-tied with the brusqueness
of many contacts, or hang up the phone only to remember that
a critical point was left out.

A well-rehearsed pitch is a possible alternative. Our recommended method is to write out what you want to say, condense
it to about twenty seconds, repeat it often, *then* transfer it to
notes.

First draft:

Hello (Mr./Ms.) _____. My name is Lester Hanover, and I
sent you a press release on something you might find
interesting. Believe it or not, I'm having a garage sale for
weekend car enthusiasts a week from next Saturday. I have an
unbelievable assortment of carburetors, body parts, brakes,
tires, batteries—in fact, I have enough stuff to build a car from
scratch, which I've done three times. I'm wondering if you did
get my release and, if so, if you might want to set up an
interview.

Revised:

Hi, this is Les Hanover, and I sent you a release on a sale I'm
having a week from Saturday, more like a party for people who
go crazy for cars and their parts. I've built three cars from
scratch myself and can give your listeners some pretty good
advice on repairs. I'm hoping we might be able to talk about it
on the air.

NOTES

1. Les Hanover.

2. Sent release.

3. Giving a sale for car enthusiasts a week from Saturday.

4. I've built three cars from scratch and can give listeners a lot of repair advice.

5. Wondering if we can talk about it on the air.

To be honest, few professional publicists have the need to pitch from notes, but most would agree that you have the attention for about fifteen seconds of a contact who's never heard of you. The purpose of translating a written pitch to notes is to avoid the stilted, singsong quality that can cause the receiver to come up with an instant dial tone. The most important step is to practice repeatedly, taking as much time as you need to get your pitch to a natural, confident rhythm.

If you receive a firm "no," be polite, get off the phone, and move immediately down the list. Do not stop once you've started booking. If the response is an "I'll think about it," make a note, wait a few days, and call again until you either hear words of refusal or interpret a tentativeness as a "no" in this contact's response repertoire. Keep calling people and you'll hear the word "yes" soon enough. When it happens, write a brief note to confirm the interview:

Ms. Betty Chuckrow
Night Talk
WOR Radio
1440 Broadway
New York, NY 10018

Dear Ms. Chuckrow:

Delighted to confirm our interview for Friday, November 23, at 3:00 P.M. I'll be arriving at 1440 Broadway sometime after 2:30, and I'll ask for you on the 23rd floor. Please feel free to call me at 222-3232 if there's any further information that might be helpful. Again, thanks for your interest. I know it will be a lot of fun.

Sincerely,

Les Hanover

The confirming note is a hedge against the all-too-common mishap of showing up and not being expected. Keep a copy of the letter in your files.

While there are many variations in the booking procedure, the structured approach, carried through for a number of hours per session, is the most effective way to get publicity. If you delegate the chore, as many do, take responsibility for your campaign and ensure that the person representing you follows the steps. They always work.

To recap, the five booking steps are:

1. Tighten mailing list.

2. Pre-call.

3. Mailing.

4. Follow-up call with well-planned pitch.

5. Confirming note.

10

Looking at Yourself

An interview is a simulation of conversation disguised as a candid exchange of ideas. True, there is a subculture of people whose professional lives depend on interviews—from talk-show assistants to movie stars—and these sleight-of-hand experts can make it look real, but don't be surprised if your own on-air discussions aren't sonic booms at the outset of your campaign. It takes practice before you can learn to regulate the pressure on your word flow, listen to a conversation's underlying rhythms, pick up the pace here, drop a bit of controversy or gossip there, come in with the host or hostess for a commercial break at the precise moment of a floor director's signal.

It is the work of master interview carpenters that we see most on television. A skilled interviewer can effect the most sincere demeanor, staring deeply into a guest's eyes while inserting the proper nods and the appropriate questions as he or she plans dinner or replays an erotic fantasy. An experienced talk-show guest can be impassioned to the point of tears, pleading the plight of impoverished children while wondering if there's a bathroom nearby and if the upcoming break will provide enough time to use it.

Does this mean that we're being had every time we observe

an interview? Far from it. The situation is artificial; the people are genuine. When Phil Donahue runs up the aisle looking for a face at which to target the top of his cordless mike, he's thinking about his topic and his show. But if he'd slammed his finger in a car door minutes before air time and the pain dominated his thinking, he would still probably be able to get through the show without his audience knowing his plight. All pros have learned to choreograph interviews with a repertoire of questions and answers that they use constantly. They've learned to tap and project from a reservoir of reality amidst the chaos of studios, remote locations, and newsrooms. Their livelihood depends on making the process look fresh every time. You're going to learn some of this magic. It's really easy.

First, you must relentlessly scrutinize your appearance. Get used to looking at yourself. Look at recent snapshots, or have some taken. Scan a full-length mirror. Have a spouse or close friend talk to you honestly about what should change. You don't have to make dramatic alterations, but you do have to take a head-to-toe inventory.

HAIR

Is this the hairstyle you really want or is it a comfortable vestige of another era that you've been meaning to update? Play around with it, trying a few new looks before making a decision. Men tend to have a more difficult time here than women, primarily because they're not as accustomed to seeking advice from those they trust.

Regardless of the style you prefer, and whether you're a man or a woman, there is one cardinal rule. Hair should be neat and out of your face at all times. The devil-may-care "casual" hairstyle is not only distracting, it is also likely to detract from your purpose in being on the show. When in doubt, lean toward understatement.

Curls are wonderful, but they should be kept trim and on the shorter side of their haircut-to-haircut growth cycle. If they get too long, the scrutiny of a closeup will make it look as if your face were under a vineyard.

Take a compact hair dryer with you to the television station. If this makes you feel vain, remember the danger of weather and what it can do to your hair. Whether you are caught in a rainstorm or are merely the victim of a sticky day in August, an unkempt hairstyle will throw you off, especially when you see yourself in the makeup mirror just before air time. You don't have to show the world you're carrying a dryer, but you should never go into a television station without one. There may be only one moment in the whole campaign when you need to slip into the rest room with it, but that one moment will produce one very deep sigh of relief.

If you're bald, can you live with it, or would you prefer a toupee? And, if you wear a toupee, level with yourself. Does the netting show? Forget what the guy who sold you the thing said about it being the same hairstyle Mick Jagger wears; Mick has his own hair and you don't. If it looks phony, get a new one or go without.

Baldness carries its own attractiveness and credibility, but only if you believe it. If you feel uncomfortable with your head, get a toupee, but don't go alone! Someone you trust has to come with you.

EYES

Many men who have never appeared on television learn that they must use makeup, and they wonder if this means eye makeup. It does not. The next paragraph is for women only.

Have you tried anything new in eye makeup lately? Are you satisfied with what you see when you look carefully? Experiment a little and take the best advice that comes down the pike, your own. You have to listen to yourself even though you need friends and their advice. Don't be so self-critical that you lose objectivity, however. Look for what really pleases you and allow yourself to enjoy it. The start of a publicity campaign is a good excuse to visit a department store for a complete facial and eye-makeup consulting session with a specialist.

We say everything with our eyes. You should practice speaking into a mirror and monitoring your eyes and eyebrows during the conversation. If you're excited about something, do your eyes register the emotion? Practice "saying things" without using words. Know your eyes and what they're capable of conveying.

Do you look at people when you speak to them, and, if so, do you hold eye contact for a socially appropriate interval? If you've never thought about that question, you're probably in great shape and there's no need to go crazy with self-consciousness at this point. But you might also have been told that you shift your eyes too much, or that you look away, conveying a demeanor that you don't feel. Now is the time to seek advice and deal honestly in your assessment of this situation. Practice holding, or not holding, eye contact during conversation. If you're a lifelong averter, take the time to learn conversational eye contact through your own practice and in the observation of others in social situations.

What about glasses? Do you think you should switch to contacts for your appearance? You might worry about glasses glaring on camera. If Woody or Steve Allen doesn't worry, why should you? Many people who look wonderful with glasses feel the need to be without them when they go on television. If it makes you feel better to change to contacts, do so. If you're going to squint or blink to achieve what you consider a better look, stick with the glasses. If glasses are part of the way you see yourself, part of your character, and cemented to your self-image, wear them.

NOSE

A lot of people don't like their noses. Don't run out and get plastic surgery, just know your nose from varying angles.

Probably the most important item to check here is whether your nose tends to shine under the high temperature conditions of a television studio. If so, you'll have to experiment with corn silk and other powder to find the right shade and dosage of makeup. This advice applies to men as well as women.

Nostril hair might need clipping before a television appearance. Check it out.

CHEEKS

Men don't like to think about makeup, and who can blame them? But ruts from adolescence that look virile or weathered can detract from credibility on camera and should now be assessed. Even the most rugged dudes use makeup on television.

Women should merely reassess at this point. Are you wearing makeup that truly flatters or are you trying to recapture a look that age has taken away? If so, what's the next look going to be like for you? Now is the time to experiment and decide.

Men should consider purchasing makeup from a department store or pharmacy offering *theatrical* makeup, for only there can they be guided in the proper direction. The person selling you the makeup will take a professional look and offer you some very sound advice. Don't be bashful about this. The person who routinely sells theatrical makeup sees men all the time. If you have to travel a few miles to find this kind of professional makeup distributor, the trip is well worth it. Most towns, however, have someone who furnishes schools and theater groups with professional advice and supplies.

A lot of people assume that a television station has a professional on hand to apply makeup to guests. Some do and some don't, and even when there is such a person present, there is no guarantee that you'll receive anything more than a cursory dusting. Don't leave makeup to chance.

MOUTH

Fear of the dentist is an international pastime. Perhaps you've been procrastinating a cleaning for fear of the doctor's scolding, or because you think one visit is going to lead to a $10,000 investment in caps. Make peace with everything but the cleaning, which is imperative at this point.

Your dentist can now offer a variety of new cosmetic techniques such as enamel bonding for chipped or discolored teeth, and he doesn't even use a needle in many cases. The best news is that technology has given us lower costs. Talk to a number of dentists if you have serious cosmetic problems. The verdict might not be as bad as you anticipate.

Women should choose lipstick carefully; bright reds and oranges are distracting, while lip gloss makes light bounce around your face. It won't be your fault. Television studios have lots of glare potential.

CHIN

Men with heavy beards are vulnerable to sinister looks, especially as the hour of 5:00 P.M. approaches. Kings, princes, and quarterbacks often shave before late-afternoon or evening television appearances, and you might have to do the same.

Check to see where your chin lands in the normal way you hold your head. Practice moving your head around to highlight it at its best.

YOUR GOOD AND BAD SIDE

Actors and actresses aren't kidding when they demand that only their best sides be photographed. Find yours and practice tilting your head in front of a mirror. Whether you are pleased with the prospect or not, you'll probably be seated to the left of a talk-show host, but it doesn't matter. If you know your face well enough, you'll be able to tilt it slightly to your advantage.

NECK

Plan to go light on neckwear. A simple gold chain or a string of pearls is preferable to a junkyard of clanging necklaces and pendants. Men have to choose between an open-shirt look or a jacket and tie, either of which is all right. The man-as-peacock look of the seventies is as far behind us now as love beads and peace signs. When in doubt, lean toward the conservative end of the dress spectrum.

UPPER TORSO

Nothing between your waist and chin should distract from the purpose of your interview. Loud shirts, plunging necklines, medallions, or busy T-shirts can throw off your whole pitch. In the event of a novelty campaign, political interview, or some other sharply focused appearance, you might even consider a T-shirt as a powerful means of free advertising, but check out a show before wearing one. You might find yourself bumped prior to air time if a producer feels that your shirt and the free plug it delivers compromise the show with the public, the FTC, or the FCC. Be guided by good taste.

WAIST

Weight is an unpleasant issue. Make a decision and stick to it. If you're overweight and not generally inclined to diet, don't make unrealistic demands upon yourself. If you enjoy the challenge of a diet and have been up and down the scales a few times, go ahead and lose. In either case, assess and accept.

Don't go out on the campaign with any reason to make body language apologies for your appearance.

LEGS

Women usually know it and men sometimes don't: Keep your knees together in the course of an interview. Don't fidget with your legs or move your feet across the floor. Put your legs in a comfortable position, feet on the floor, and sit there until you receive the signal to leave the set.

CLOTHING

Now's the time to shop. Dress to convey the image you want to project. If you're hard at work to right a social wrong and wear a mink to the interview, your outfit will be remembered and your message lost. Watch talk shows again and resurrect your notebook.

Notice that middle-aged people in conservative gray convey an aging, weak impression. Someone the same age in a medium blue looks ready to run a marathon. Call your partner or someone you really trust in for another consultation and consider the following traditionally held views on television dress:

- Extremes of any kind should be avoided—too light washes you out, too dark tends to exaggerate facial features. White shirts are worn nowadays by television anchormen, but they have an army of lighting technicians. In a local television or cable interview, they may not have the expertise to make you look good in white. If the lighting is wrong, the white will glare and the director will shoot you in an unflattering facial closeup.

- Bright reds and shocking pink look better off camera than on the air because they tend to frizz up and sometimes "burn" an image that remains on screen after the director has punched up the next shot.

- Dark greens can make you look downright scary. Lighter, minty shades can also reflect an unflattering pallor to a carefully prepared makeup job. While some television personalities manage to look good in green, our advice is to avoid it.

- Wear an understated pinstripe if you favor stripes at all. Bold stripes sometimes distort.

- Those who favor a tweedy, elbow-patched look have to be careful about their choice of patterned sport jacket. Pronounced herringbone or tweeds will appear to jump off your sleeve and into the air when the camera moves.

- Large-patterned plaids can create a make-believe weight problem or add to a real one.

In short, your color scheme has to be reminiscent of Goldilocks's porridge: not too light, not too dark, not too anything. It certainly must not be too cheap. This isn't the time to cut back on the budget. Tans, blues, and medium browns are especially effective, and you should feel free to choose a cut that flatters you. Make sure that the fit is exquisite, even if it never has been in your life.

SHOES

Scuffed shoes are always out. If you are inclined to allow the luster to dull, you have a little something to unlearn. In most cases your shoes will not be seen, but they should look great anyway.

COSMETIC ITEMS

Toupees. How often have you seen one that is really attractive? Most of them look like badly made hats. Unless you're prepared to invest heavily, your natural hairline would be considered preferable.

Hair Transplants. They're great if you're blessed with the ten to fifteen grand or more that will be required for the process. Otherwise, remember that a lot of people think bald is sexy.

Dermabrasion. Dermabrasion is a relatively uncomplicated dermatological operation that helps remedy the sad ravages of adolescent acne. If your face is scarred from your high school years, check out the possibility with a dermatologist or plastic surgeon. The procedure can usually be done in the office.

Makeup. Our position is that men should be concerned with only two types of makeup: pancake and corn-silk. A well-stocked drugstore will help you with the selection of a pancake that matches your skin. Take a friend when you go, and carry the makeup with you whenever you're doing television. It is applied with a wet sponge and a piece of cloth.

Even more convenient is corn-silk powder that can be applied quickly and with little trace of a "made-up" look that makes many men feel uncomfortable. Whichever you choose, be sure to use some kind of makeup. You will look better and all the macho guys wear it.

Women who do not know how to apply makeup are a rarity in our society. Rules rarely change for television, but you might treat yourself to a facial and a makeup consultation from a department or beauty store specialist. Otherwise, remember to add enough time in your schedule to keep it all fresh and pay a little more attention to eye makeup than you would for a normal, nonpublic meeting.

WEIGHT AND THE CAMERA

You will frequently hear that a television camera adds ten pounds to your appearance. Sometimes it does not add any weight, and sometimes it adds more. Make your decision on weight early on and live with it. If you just can't get rid of the pounds, resolve to be so damned good that no one will notice. By and large, the camera does add weight, and there isn't anything you can do about it. The camera does lie, though. Some people, regardless of their physical excesses or deprivations, experience a miraculous alchemy when the red light blinks on. They look wonderful. No one knows the why or how of this, but anyone who ever spent more than a day around a studio has stories of Plain Janes or Sad Sacks who radiate a glow on camera. If you're not in this category, pretend you are.

TEETH

As we mentioned earlier, see your dentist for a good cleaning before doing any publicity appearances, even radio. Touch-ups can be made with an electric toothbrush and tooth polish or bicarbonate of soda, although if your teeth are bonded be sure to ask your dentist before applying any abrasive substance.

Many new cosmetic techniques can be completed in a single session, without anesthesia and for considerably less than the cost of capping. If your teeth are chipped, misformed, or discolored, treat yourself to at least one consultation with a dentist who is abreast of recent cosmetic developments.

11
Listening to Yourself

You might wonder where radio people find their exaggerated announcing qualities and whether you should do anything to make your voice sound like theirs. No way. They sound like that because professionalism in radio demands the shedding of regional accents; while doing so, they often pick up an announcer sound that is as difficult to escape as the accent itself. You'll sometimes find that radio people announce everything—the taste of the punch, the color of your dress, the falling of a leaf. This you don't need.

Your conversational resonance is far more important than any effort at standardization. If you have a stammer, lisp, or other serious impediment, only a certified speech therapist can help you. There are books on phonetics that will rid you of your accent if you someday want to do so and are prepared to spend a year or more practicing on a daily basis. For now, check out the following hints.

Your voice is a gust of wind that becomes sound by traveling through a vibrating larynx. You can trace the entire path of your voice by putting your finger on your neck as you open wide and say, "Aaaaahhhhh," just as you would if a doctor were checking your tonsils. Feel around for the vibration, and you'll have the larynx. The mouth and nasal passages serve as resonating caverns.

Your tongue taps voice into speech in an amazing concert with your teeth and lips. Pay attention to how these articulating organs work together. Notice that your *S*'s hiss through the teeth while *M* and *N* sounds find air only after traveling through your nose. Stick your tongue out (preferably with no one else in the room) and try to make an *S*. Hold your nose while attempting any word with *M* or *N*.

Nervousness reverberates through your system from the larynx to the final sounds of articulated speech. When you feel uneasy before an interview, try breathing deeply before going on—not an exaggerated intake but a quiet and slow passage of air. Don't rush it.

Practice opening your mouth wide as you let the vowels bounce around in there. Aaaaaaaaay . . . Eeeeeeeeee . . . etc. Read aloud as you enunciate every syllable. These exercises won't get you voice-over work in New York, but they will accustom you to the sound of your own speaking rhythm.

Chapter 13 will help you develop a media act. For now, listen to yourself in conversation for a while, hard as that will be at first. Do you take too long in getting to a point? Do you trail off? Do you retreat when a louder person interrupts? Are you sometimes too quick to interrupt yourself? How well do you really listen? It's homework time again.

1. Take every question that could possibly come up for your primary booking angle, and type each on its own card. Have a friend ask them at random, shuffling the cards before each session.

2. Tape yourself during these sessions, and make yourself listen carefully. There's a better-than-average chance that you're going to hate this, but do it anyway. Most people have an impression of their vocal selves that differs dramatically

from reality. You might find a regional accent that you never knew about, and chances are that the voice you've always heard is more suave and melodious than that terrifying bray the tape recorder is now claiming belongs to you. It takes time, but you'll get to a point of détente and start to coexist with the sound of your speech. Be comforted in knowing that those wonderful voices that pitch shampoo or beer are the product of many years of training—and often their owners still cringe.

3. Work out a list of adversary questions, being as rude as possible with yourself and your primary booking angle. If you think there's nothing controversial in your subject matter, consider the possibilities in the examples we know well:

- Mrs. Barnes, don't you think you're denigrating your profession and your position in the community with the blatant commercialism of your press release on tax loopholes?

- Mr. Hanover, you might call it a garage sale for auto enthusiasts. I say you're a junk merchant without a peddler's license.

- Mrs. Parnell, you're really selling teeth-rotting, sugar-based junk food to raise uniforms for young people, and you're setting a horrible example. Isn't there some other way you can find the money for the Little League?

- Mr. Carter, the deregulation of the phone company has unleashed a swarm of fly-by-night phone hucksters. Are you one of them?

- A restaurant serving only pasta sounds disgusting, Ms. Wright, if I may inject a personal comment.

Most of your interviews are going to be conducted by nice people. Be ready for the rare occasions when insult replaces reason.

4. Have your partner ask the questions and interrupt every answer you provide, changing the subject to a totally irrelevant conversational track. Your job is to return to your primary booking angle within two minutes.

5. Switch places with your partner and ask the questions yourself. Then repeat the steps in exercise 4 as you take the role of the interrupter.

6. With your partner asking the questions, answer them as:

- A loudmouth with no interest in the subject matter beyond its conveyance of his own ego needs.

- A supershy individual who can't get a sentence out without stammering.

- A back-slapping comic who makes a joke out of everything.

- A pedantic pseudointellectual who turns every sentence into a philosophical treatise.

- A malaprop who misinterprets questions and comes up with non sequiturs for answers.

The purpose of this chapter is for you to observe. Don't fret about problems you've found. They'll work themselves out in time, if you make the commitment to their solutions. Our purpose for now is to help you know more about the you that others see and hear. Pay as much attention to yourself as possible, stressing the positive. In that you don't really have time to completely overhaul your persona, make an attempt to isolate what impresses you about yourself (and do allow yourself to be impressed), so that you'll soon be able to use these strengths to your advantage.

12

Problem Interviews

Most of your interviewers will be serious, competent individuals who are well positioned in their trade. There are exceptions that you should know about. This chapter provides an overview of interviewer types, some of whom should be in mortuary work or another field where they can cause no embarrassment and do no harm. But limelight, even at the most local level, is addictive, and these characters will generally tell you that they stumbled into the radio station or newspaper office as children en route to another destination such as the library, where they hoped to pick up a book on vivisection. They got into the business by mistake, and they brag about it. You are about to be part of a lifelong compounding of that mistake.

Not to worry. Anyone with a by-line or access to a broadcast transmitter is important to your campaign. Most problem interviewers suffer primarily from insecurity born of vanity and some inner voice that tells them their careers will not, and should not, go any further. You can control the situation by knowing what you're up against. Meet the cast.

BARBIE

Her hair is reminiscent of Miss America 1955. She dresses up for her interviews, courtesy of a local boutique that gets a plug in the program's closing credits. Her teeth glisten like Chiclets beneath a shade of lipstick that is a trifle too crimson. Barbie didn't get to read your material and confesses just before you go on that she prefers not to know too much about her guests for fear of losing the freshness of a moment. As a result, you're there to talk about saving money on long-distance calls and she thinks the segment is about handling obscene callers or developing a pleasant telephone manner.

Solution. It's her show, and she can take it anywhere she wants. Look for your opportunity to glide toward the plug as gracefully as possible. For example:

BARBIE: So, Bob, as an executive with Call-Maker, what advice can you give me on obscene phone calls?

BOB: Actually, Barbie, I'd advise your listeners to talk with a specialist we have at Call-Saver who knows far more than I about dealing with the problem. Her name is Helena Reed, and she can be reached between nine and five by calling 555-3535. I've developed another area of expertise, and that is to save anyone with a telephone up to 60 percent on long-distance calls.

Of course, if you do know something about the topic, so much the better. If not, don't try to fudge. Barbie will often misrepresent your product or organization, as she did above. When that happens, try to avoid interrupting her or saying, "I must correct you, Barbie." Simply work in the correction within the context of the discussion as soon as possible. When you introduce a fresh topic, Barbie, or any interviewer, has little choice but to run with it. Meanwhile, you have little choice but to run with Barbie, for she represents thousands of viewers who take her a lot more seriously than we do.

KEN

This guy has a Glen Campbell hairstyle, a John Denver smile, and the intelligence of a waffle iron. He's there because he's cute, and he'll spend the segment reminding everyone of that fact. He smiles flirtatiously at the camera and looks right through you. His reaction to your subject matter will vary from inappropriate jokes to feigned interest in all the wrong places.

Solution. See solution to "Barbie."

BARBIE AND KEN

Lucky you when this dynamic duo interviews you together on a morning talk show. Between making plugs for restaurants that give them free food and boutiques that supply their wardrobes, interrupting each other, dropping names of the eminent community members who greet them at the club, and taking commercial breaks, they will barely notice that you're on the set.

Solution. These people desperately crave respect, and you would do well to give it to them if you can do so in a non-patronizing way. In a world where materialism is often the scorecard of position, their salaries, lecture fees, freebies, ribbon cuttings, and other emcee functions often earn these stooges six figures apiece every year. They've done something right, even if that something happens not to be their jobs. Barbie and Ken want short, punchy answers to which they will respond by tripping over each other to give out the plug information. You could do worse.

MINI-MIKE

This interviewer has a hard time living with the notion that Mike Wallace is in New York while he's in a radio station between the Sears Auto Center and K-Mart. He knows that fame is a phone call away, if only he can show CBS that he has the right stuff.

You walk in on a Monday, the day *Broadcasting* magazine comes out with its help-wanted display ads for slots in the industry's major leagues. You don't know it, but your interview is going to be part of an audition tape that Mini-Mike is, damn it, going to get right this time. He makes no distinction between hard and soft interviews. If you're there for something as noble as curing diabetes or an orphanage fund raiser, Mike will be looking for controversy:

"But how much of this money do the children actually see? Is there a shopping trip for them to spend some of it, or do you keep it all and spend it on bureaucratic waste?"

And that's if he likes you.

Solution. Be calm, for you're dealing with a moron. Buy a little composing time by saying, "I'm glad you asked that question, Mike." Then hold your ground. Throw a statistic in his face, prefaced by, "As you know, Mike . . ." or "As you may have read in *The New York Times*, Mike . . ." Regardless of the statistic's obscurity, he'll often pretend to know. Remember not to lie. There's always a listener who will catch you at it. Mini-Mike will never get his call from New York, but you might consider encouraging him to apply for a job at a bigger station during the commercial breaks when the two of you are stuck with nothing to do but banter. Tell him he gets right to the point. Mini-Mikes often attract sizable local followings, and, unlike the next person on our agenda, they are blustery but not especially dangerous.

THE TERRORIST

The Terrorist interviewer has fantasies about buzzards and your carcass. Sometimes it's an alter-ego thing where the kid who was bullied grows up to kick sand in the face of every adult on the beach. The mike is a power elixir.

In other cases, the Terrorist is a lifelong risk taker and you're part of the run. Every decade in the history of broadcasting seems to have produced a brief need for a few of these fire starters; the air waves are littered with their memories.

Whatever the psychology, the Terrorist will insult, lie, distort facts, and generally take whatever measures he deems necessary to demean your case.

Solution. Arguments sometimes make good broadcasting, so you'll have to put aside your biases to determine whether you're dealing with a contrary person or a genuine Terrorist (of which there are very few). If so, there is only one solution: Politely excuse yourself and leave the studio.

DR. SENSITIVE

Ten years ago, radio people discovered that certain talk-show hosts could get high ratings by extracting confessions from members of the listening audience. These confidants were most popular in the middle of the day when housewives would discuss extramarital affairs, frustration with the drudgery of their lives, missed careers, and impending divorces.

Like so many of life's refreshing changes, the format soon became topheavy with excess. Hosts, usually male, knew where their bread was buttered: Skip the career frustrations and child-rearing problems and get on with the X-rated stuff. Pressure groups and the FCC soon brought racy radio to a G-rated halt.

Programmers have now figured out a way to revive and legitimize a trace of their early seventies bonanza. Hire a host with an M.D. or Ph.D., tone down the sex (or at least couch it in professional jargon), and shift the scope to *relationships*, the biggest buzz word of the eighties to date.

In fairness, call-in shrinks are often performing a valuable public service, for they are bound by a rigid code of professional ethics not to perform psychotherapy on the air. Often, a rapist will seek help instead of a victim, or a battering husband will take the thirty-second pause that makes the difference between a violent domestic incident and an evening of truce. No major market is without its share of prevented suicides. But there is also a minority category of questionable practitioners who make you wonder if perhaps the "Dr." in front of their names came from a mail-order house.

In many markets, psychologists work daily air shifts and expand their scope beyond the usual touch and feel. You are most likely to meet Dr. Sensitive if you're promoting a drug hot line, a school program, a social agency, or even a commercial establishment such as a dating service.

Dr. Sensitive greets you with mounds of compassion, so much of it that you'll probably find yourself gagging on the empathy. The eyes beg you to confess.

"I want to know how you *feel* about yourself, how it is for *you*. Will you share your experience with us?"

Sharing. You feel as if your methodology for monitoring your soul has to be passed around like water in a desert. You think you'll fail on the show if you don't admit to at least one misdemeanor in your moral life.

Solution. It's not difficult to come up against one of these broadcast monuments to sixtiesspeak by mistake. If you find yourself being asked once too often to emote on cue, you can always say, "Your question, Dr. Sensitive, is one that forces me to explore some feelings that I seem not to have access to at the moment. May we move instead to another topic?" Or, "I don't think a public forum is the best place for me to discuss this."

Above all, confess nothing. You're not talking to Dr. Sensitive in a therapeutic environment. There may be a hundred thousand listeners who will remember your appearance long after the good doctor has forgotten your name.

THE CATATONIC

Suppose you've been through a dozen or more interviews already and your act is tight. You've danced your way through various lines of questioning, sometimes with difficulty but ultimately with triumph. You've seen it all, you think, until you meet the Catatonic.

The Catatonic asks you a question, then sinks into a coma from which only an act of war can arouse him. You give the usual answer and take the usual pause as you await a follow-up question. Because the system hasn't failed you before, you have no reason to expect what's about to happen. You find that little hairs on the back of your neck are standing at attention. He's not saying anything.

The Catatonic is sometimes deliberate, sometimes inept, but always jarring. Mini-Mike and Dr. Sensitive become comparative love objects as you fumble around for something to fill the ether. They at least talked. You weren't out there alone. Dan Greenburg, the best-selling author of *How to Be a Jewish Mother*, his first book, recalls meeting a Catatonic on the road.

"So, you're from New York, Dan?"

"Yes, I am, Ed."

"What's that French restaurant?"

"Well, there are about two thousand five hundred of them in New York, Ed."

"You know the one I mean."

"Er . . . Lutèce?"

Pause.

"Le Cirque? La Grenouille? La Caravelle?"

"Nope." Pause.

Greenburg proceeded to run his considerable knowledge of Manhattan eateries past his interviewer, receiving either a pause or a shake of the head after each one.

"It was obvious to me," he recalls seventeen years later, "that I wasn't going to be interviewed until I stumbled on the name of that restaurant. Luckily, I hit it."

Because of the medium's longer programs, the Catatonic is more likely to be a radio interviewer than a television talker or a press person. You're never safe until you learn how to handle the situation.

Solution. The Catatonic offers either a wonderful opportunity or the most difficult interview of your campaign, depending on your ability to recover. You're on the guillotine if you're in the midst of "tour glaze," a phenomenon that settles over interviewees like a cast-iron mold. You become so accustomed to the same questions that your answers become rote. You've trained yourself to respond to questions with the concise and punchy answers that are the center beam of virtually all interviews. With a Catatonic, the rules change. You have to take over.

In the next chapter you'll learn more about solidifying your on-air persona by first developing large blocks of conversation that are eventually whittled to fit the ordinary chatter of your interviews. The Catatonic provides an exception where you return to large paragraphs of speech.

You're not as bad off as you might initially believe. First, take a second to breathe deeply and get your bearings. If he's going to pause, it is not your responsibility to fill. The deep breath does not mean a sharp, audible intake of air but an instant of quietude that results in a recognition that no one is going to hit you with a club. It's your show now. Say what you like.

Focus on your primary booking angle and start speaking. For a few seconds, you'll probably want to race through your material, but to do so is to succumb to a panic impulse. Instead, relax and enjoy the moment. Ask him a few questions that are pertinent to the material.

"Bob, do you spend more than fifteen dollars a month on long-distance calls?"

"Yes, I believe I do." (Catatonics tend to come up for air when questions are asked of them.)

"Then Call-Saver can cut your telephone bills in half."

Continue running things until the Catatonic resurfaces or tells you that time is up. If he doesn't, it's your show and you have a new career!

THE PAL

Press people who have deadlines but no air time to fill are adept at an interviewing technique designed to gain your confidence. They smile and nod supportively, encouraging you to say more without actually telling you that they approve. Some of our best investigative reporting occurs this way.

The Pal is a threat only if there are things you don't want publicized. Political people and others in public life know that a chance remark made during an interview can become the basis for tomorrow's headlines and perhaps the end of the whole ride. Ask Earl Butz or James Watt.

If you are being interviewed on a topic of little controversy, the Pal is merely making full use of the luxury of nonshowmanship. He or she doesn't have to be on and isn't. Enjoy the technique but don't get overconfident, lest you find yourself tomorrow afternoon saying, "Gee, did I say that? I couldn't have."

Solution. Reporters operate on an "on the record," "off the record" basis in order to cultivate sources whose rights they fiercely protect. If you are gaining rapport with a reporter and wish to go "off the record" or offer a statement "for background only," say so and you're almost guaranteed not to be quoted. If there is a tape recorder running, as there usually is nowadays, ask that it be turned off.

If the Pal in your life is known for inaccuracies, or if you're dealing with ultrasensitive subject matter, bring your own tape recorder to the interview, making sure that it goes on and off in synch with his. For most campaigns, such a measure is unnecessary, but when in doubt, record and rest.

Treat a reporter as you would a live mike. Don't drink during an interview unless you've had a lot of experience, and even then, one is plenty. A recent deluge of movies portraying press people as foxlike ogres who ruin careers with careless reporting of sketchy information would indicate that the Pal is out to get you. In reality, such is not the case. But if you get careless and start blowing a little hot air around in the belief that it makes "good copy," or if you tell your interviewer something you don't want in the paper without so specifying before blurting it out, you're fair game. Be open but professional.

THE INTERRUPTER

The Interrupter has his private hell, and you can't see it. He fears that his show will drag, that you'll talk too long, and the momentum will dissipate. The fear manifests itself in excessive interruption of his guests. You make half a remark, and he's on top of you with another question or his own remark. You are so riddled with questions that you are eventually unable to remember what you've already said. You just wish it would end.

Solution. The Interrupter is like a carnival finger trap where the harder you tug, the tighter the bind. The more you give in and let him change the subject every fifteen seconds, the more desperate he'll be to jump around.

First, have the confidence to stick to your material even if you have to dice it into shorter chunks. Respond briefly to each change he tries to initiate, but quickly move back to where you were. Sometimes you'll have to come right out and tell him that you'll answer that question in a few seconds, but first you have to settle the issue at hand.

There is an optimum rhythm for interrupters that you'll quickly find if you don't panic. Generally, he's only trying to counteract the possibility of a monotone, and, given the pedantic nature of many interviewees, one can hardly blame him. Keep your focus on your primary booking angle and you'll soon find that he'll interrupt a little less and probably won't change the subject at all until you're ready. The Interrupter likes a seesaw momentum, and if the ride is a little fast-paced, that's show biz. Keep your cool, and you'll have a good time here.

THE CALLERS

Watch out when the host says, "Hello, you're on the air," because you don't know what sort of mutant managed to get through the screening process. The profane callers are the easiest, for they are cut off seven seconds before their nastiness can reach the transmission line. More jarring are the blunt, bottom-line types who are apt to ask you anything.

Solution. If you have not yet listed every negative question you can think of, do so. Add these to the list, and develop some spare-tire responses:

"I think the idea is stupid and so are you."

(If that's what you think, madam, I'm not going to convince you otherwise. Thank you for calling.)

"The Bible says that people like you will burn in hell."

(Don't discuss the Bible with a caller even if you hold a doctorate in theology. Politely inform the caller that he's entitled to his own interpretation of Scripture, but you're on the program for other purposes.)

"Communists love to see people like you who are wrecking our society."

(I'll remember that the next time I see a Communist, sir. Or, They prefer demagogues like yourself, sir, they're easier to control.)

"You belong in jail."

(I don't happen to think so, ma'am.)

"Would you want your children doing what you suggest?"

(I wouldn't be suggesting it if I weren't prepared to have my child do it.)

Even the most bush-league talk-show host has learned to cut people off quickly when they become abusive. When you're in doubt, look toward your interviewer. Never take bait and always avoid sophistry. For example:

"Do you believe in evolution?"

"What's it got to do with day-care centers, sir?"

"Just answer yes or no, do you believe in evolution?"

This type of caller has used the same sort of syllogistic reasoning a thousand times or more. Don't walk into it.

"I'm here to express my view of employer-sponsored day-care centers, and I'll be glad to answer any questions you have on that topic and that topic only, sir."

We must stress that in most cases your interviewer will be on the cut-off switch at the first syllable from a lunatic caller. Some of your most touching moments will come from the grass-roots help you offer listeners through the dialogue you provide on talk radio or television. Be prepared for problems, but don't let apprehension of a long shot rob you of this satisfaction. That premise may be applied to the entire spectrum of problem interviewers. They'll always be around, but they're definitely in the minority.

13

Developing a Media Act

You will be asked the same questions constantly, and you will provide virtually every interviewer with the same set of answers. Your task is to make it look fresh each time out.

Stand-up comics spend years developing routines that are timed perfectly for laughter. The singer you see on national television has usually practiced each note and gesture to perfection. You don't have that kind of time to develop your "act," but you don't need it either. You do, however, need a few practice sessions with your material in order to avoid looking uninterested in your own subject matter.

1. Repeat Chapter 11's list of pertinent questions into a tape recorder. For now, just read the questions. Are they all there?

2. Repeat the answers without asking the questions themselves. Do not write out your answers but say them aloud, play them back, and say them aloud again.

3. Practice going down the list of questions and repeating them until you know them extremely well. Then answer them, a hundred times if necessary. You might think such repetition

will make you stale, but the opposite is more likely to
happen: If you know your stuff so well that the answers are
ingrained, you'll be freer to express these responses with
more variety later. Not everyone agrees with this
philosophy, but try it very hard and see how you feel.

4. If a partner is available, he or she should also ask you
   questions repeatedly, but this time a variation in each
   answer should be demanded of you. It doesn't have to be a
   vastly creative departure from your previous answers—it
   probably shouldn't be, in fact—but the answers should now
   vary a bit. Tape these sessions and take the time to play
   them back.

5. You should now have a block of material that you can
   produce if an interviewer says, "Tell me about yourself,"
   and disappears for fifteen minutes. You are also at a point
   where you'll want to skip this nonsense, especially if you've
   been doing interviews already. *Don't skip it.* There are
   hundreds of cases in your own neighborhood where people
   find that they can't progress to the more competitive shows
   because they became overconfident, or overimpressed, with
   their ability to handle interviews. Rehearse your block of
   material the way you would rehearse a speech. Know it the
   way an army recruit knows his rifle. Rehearse it with
   questions, then try it without them. Time yourself and see
   how long you can talk about your topic without any
   interruptions.

6. If you can start talking about your primary booking angle
   and progress to your secondary angles nonstop for fifteen or
   more minutes, you're ready to continue. If not, go back and
   review until you know everything so well that you dream
   about it. Now you're ready to whittle. Get a friend
   involved, and ask that person to interrupt you at every
   available interval in the material. Be sure that there are not

a lot of non sequiturs here, but a few are more than acceptable. For example:

FRIEND: Tell me about your company, Al.

YOU: Well, Fred, I started it about six months ago . . .

FRIEND: Did you fly in from New York?

YOU: Yes, Fred, I did. Anyway, the company comes in response to a need I perceived in the leather goods marketplace . . .

FRIEND: What need? You surely can't be telling me that there's something *new* in leather usage.

You will do serious damage to your prospects of being on a television show again if you cannot translate shoptalk into conversation. Steve Friedman, executive producer of NBC's *Today* show, considers a potential guest's most important quality being "able to answer questions quickly and in language the 'common' person could understand." He also sums up the cardinal rule for any potential guest in two words: "Be lively."

We have asked you to develop your material to the point at which everyone in your life, including you, is bored with it. You are becoming tedious in a world that prosecutes tedium more vigorously than most crimes. But mastering material is the first step in developing a sound media act. Most people believe such mastery is the final step. That is why you will probably be the best guest on the talk-show couch. If you have properly rehearsed at this point, put it all away and watch a little television.

Whom do you resemble? Most famous people have a "look" that represents a segment of the population. Now is the time to be influenced by the person who represents your type. Assimilate this person's professional qualities without doing an impersonation. Rich Little you're not. But you can watch various types on television and see how they respond to questions and how they provide their answers. Just watch. Keep in mind the person you believe most resembles your style as you proceed with the next phases of your emerging act.

BRIGHTENING YOUR MATERIAL

Now that you can answer every question you'll be asked without thinking about it, it's time to seriously evaluate your conversational qualities. What have people always told you about yourself?

While we are all a chameleonic blend of personalities that reflect the many influences of our growth, we usually have a single aura of temperament that performers refer to as *attitude*. Attitude is your overall persona—droll, serious, funny, witty, taciturn, aggressive, or whatever. Transferring your everyday attitude into stage presence is beyond our scope here, but, if you think about it, you'll recognize that you do have one selling quality that puts you across. It is the strengthening of your attitude that will transform your material from so many nouns and verbs to a dazzling sales pitch, if you open yourself up and make peace with who you really are. The following is a guide to a few prevailing personality types with a bit of advice on how to use attitude to present your material more effectively.

Serious. People who convey a serious public attitude are forever being told to "lighten up," crack a few jokes, and have a good time. In publicity, a serious demeanor is welcome. A somber or gloomy personality is a different story, but if you are serious, go with it and be glad. There are too many would-be comics on the circuit and not enough straightforward individuals whose sense of humor is confined to nonpublic occasions. The world turns on the shoulders of serious people. Who wants to see a cabinet member doing *shtick?*

The serious personality, however, is not excused from the

responsibility of avoiding boredom in a presentation. He or she is more vulnerable to it than other types. Practice projecting the enthusiasm that brought you and your subject matter together, avoid long or technical answers, and take pride in the methodical conveyance of ideas that has probably earned you the respect of your colleagues.

Shy. Shyness is a rotten handle until one learns to use it. Then it becomes one of the most attractive traits in the galaxy. No one seems to be able to resist a shy person who has replaced tentativeness with determination. You know what your enemies are—lack of eye contact, halting speech, and a tendency to waffle in conversation. But mastery of shyness in public is almost an everyday occurrence. There are debating champions who can pummel any opponent but don't know what to say in the intimacy of a conversation. Top-forty disc jockeys sometimes stammer when they get off the air, and many politicians simply can't operate on a one-to-one level. Many famous people claim to be shy. They have harnessed their bashful qualities and turned them into a public asset. If you've come this far, you probably can, too. Plunge ahead.

Loud. Some people speak with too much volume. They often come from generations of ancestors who spoke with too much volume. Loud is one of the least endearing attitudes. Even nice people who put too much diaphragm into their speech are referred to as "loudmouths." Worse, they don't always know they're loud, and, if they do know, they don't know what to do about it.

Assuming that you've been told that you're a mite loud and that you're committed to accepting it, there's some good news. Loud commands attention. You may speak with a natural authority that others have to develop, and in your efforts to tone down, be careful not to surrender that vocal conviction.

A permanent effort toward quieting your voice is a job for a speech therapist. For the limited, nonclinical scope of a publicity campaign, call that friend back into the room and have her or him tell you when your voice is at the approximate speaking level of the rest of the world. Then, tone it down and practice with the tape recorder. There is little else you can do.

Humorous. There's way too much pressure to be funny. Any professional comic will tell you that the public side of a "natural" wit is useless without more stage experience than almost anyone can imagine. Maybe you can walk into a barbershop, crack a few jokes, and cause the whole place to fall headfirst into the rinsing sinks. When that happens, which is probably often, you fantasize about playing Vegas for six figures a week. But when you go on television, you may find the humor that always got you through isn't going over.

Humor will constantly aid you in your presentation, but you should treat it with the mixture of awe and fear with which a child regards a lighted match. Don't tell jokes. If you've heard a good one, your listeners probably will be able to lip-synch the punch line. Our advice is to start out with a straight approach and see if your naturally funny demeanor shines through. If so, you're en route to heaven. If not, you won't embarrass yourself.

Perky. Perkiness is good as long as it doesn't slide into labored cuteness. If you are crisp from the moment the alarm goes off, the chances are excellent that your enthusiasm will sell your material. Your homework is to study those television guests who are just too adorable, too self-impressed, and positive to the point where you think you're going to become ill if you hear one more platitude. Learn from these people, then have a great time.

Gruff. Gruff is like shy; when played well, it is irresistible. A little gravel in the voice, a jaded view that fools no one in its effort to conceal an underlying decency, and moments of genuine warmth will sell well for you. If your attitude is gruff, be sure to twinkle a bit lest you come off as an irascible proselytizer.

Abrasive. Most of us can admire a little gruffness, but few would care to be regarded as abrasive. Are you regarded that way? It isn't always such a horrible thing, especially in business or law, where people don't succeed by displaying the compassion of a nondirective psychotherapist. In publicity, abrasiveness can be a real plus in a panel discussion where some opinionated mutant is dominating the conversation. For the most part, however, you're not going to sell anything until you ask those closest to you how you're coming over and make some very serious decisions on what to eliminate from your approach.

Sweet. Sweet people are forever being consoled with the notion that honey catches more flies than vinegar. That's fine, if you want to catch flies. If your sweetness comes from a heartfelt, other-directed desire to give, everything's great. If you believe yourself to be sweet because you're afraid to be otherwise, admit it to yourself and try to enjoy the ride. You could certainly pick up a book on assertiveness training or attend a seminar, but that is up to you. The most important—indeed, the only selling—attitude in a publicity campaign is honesty.

THE ALTER EGO

You may be one of the lucky people who gets to play opposite your type when you go out to do publicity. If you're meek, you might become aggressive on camera, or if you're a monster in the boardroom, publicity may bring out the pussycat in you. This has to happen naturally and as the result of a genuine part of your personality peeping through for a little air. Don't try to fake it. Either it happens or it doesn't.

Now call your friend back for a few final sessions with the flash cards. Shuffle them well and put yourself through a rapid-fire session with questions, this time keeping your attitude locked in the back room of your consciousness. Don't act. Let it flow naturally and allow your friend to tell you if you're conveying your optimum demeanor. With enough practice, you will be.

14
Radio Interviews

You probably already know that radio is our most accessible interview medium. If you plan a campaign of any substance, radio stations will be as familiar to you as the front seat of your car.

In a city of three commercial television stations and one PBS affiliate, you might do a single TV appearance in either a seven-minute guest shot or a ninety-second news feature. The same day should find you on the radio four or five times if you hang in and make the proper follow-up calls. You can't always get on television or into print, but anywhere on the globe, and at any hour of the day, you will be able to get on the radio. Consider it home.

ABOUT MODERN RADIO

Nearly a century after its theoretical basis prompted experimentation, radio remains a technical marvel. Your voice is converted into electrical energy, sent into space at the speed of light, captured by a receiver, and passed through speakers as sound.

Radio's primary role today is found in its immediate local

coverage. When the snow flies and there's going to be no school tomorrow, when the Cessna is lost in the woods near the airport, when the high school basketball team makes the state play-offs, radio people are there with the story. Major-market regional stations cover a wider geography, and "local" sports might be defined in professional terms, but the theme is the same.

People take radio very personally. The small stations may be amateurish when measured against the smoothies in Big Town, but when you appear on "Open Mike," "Live Wire," "Express Your Opinion," or whatever name they have for the local call-in show, you're apt to be facing an interviewer whose status in the community is more lustrous than that of any political or religious leader. People set their watches by him (or her, just as often), name their children in his honor, and keep a note pad by the radio to jot down anything he deems important.

Small- and medium-market stations are populated by two groups, the locals and the floaters. The typical floater comes into a community, gets a small apartment, and starts sending audition tapes to larger markets before he even knows where the Seven-Eleven can be found. That he would aspire to the six-figure salary of a major-market personality over the pocket change of a local station is no disgrace. If your campaign is repeated next year, you will probably find the same people in larger radio stations. Learn to keep tabs on who interviews you, write notes, and show an interest in your radio interviewers. This is not always an easy task.

Because small-market radio is the bottom rung of professional show business, it attracts a disproportionate array of egomaniacs, introverts looking for a spark of confidence, and misfits with a dark side you hope never to see. Such is the case in any creative endeavor, but in local radio the desperation somehow seems sadder. Many of the people you'll meet aren't going to make it, and they know it.

On the positive side is a delicious sense of camaraderie and a lot of people who *are* going to make it. Radio is a career start for journalists, entertainers, writers, directors, producers, and political, religious, and business leaders. They have one very important consideration in common. Jobs often end quickly in radio.

Because radio people are on the air live, the two-weeks' notice that is the birthright of civilized people everywhere is not always a part of the station routine. The job often ends right after an air shift, the severance check is handed out, and the announcer leaves immediately. In major markets, unions and contracts protect against such practices, or at least make it financially difficult on management. It all sounds inordinately cruel, but radio people accept the danger as part of the exciting game they play. If you want to throw a balanced dinner party with chitchat bouncing to a variety of issues, be careful about inviting two radio people. They love what they do and can't stop talking about it.

RADIO INTERVIEW LENGTH

Aside from news feature interviews, which are usually short, radio offers the luxury of a long conversation. You're free to express yourself, sell your pitch, and perhaps answer questions from listeners.

The most dangerous element of radio interviews is that they encourage ponderousness in us. Keep your answers short and crisp while showing interest in your interviewer. Don't feel that you have to stay with a single topic just because it happens to be what you're selling.

EVALUATING YOUR RADIO INTERVIEW

"Does this stuff really sell?" is the question publicists hear all the time from their clients. There are a few thumbnail facts that might assist in your assessment of a radio station's capacity to reach listeners. You should do as many radio interviews as you can, but some are much more effective than others.

AM STATIONS

Unless you're planning to climb a tower, the technical difference between AM and FM is of little consequence to you. Here are a few facts that tell you a little about the station you're visiting:

- Frequency refers to an AM station's spot on the dial—540 to 1600 (these numbers refer to cycles per second of the radio wave and are expressed in kilohertz, or kHz). Although there are a number of exceptions to the rule, the signals with better range are found to the left of 1200, with the smaller, more local stations operating between 1200 and 1600.

- Power is as important as frequency in determining the clout of a station. The AM power range runs from a scant 100 watts to the 50,000-watt giant stations in major cities. A station in a medium market with 1,000 or 5,000 watts will do very well for you. In a major market, anything with a transmitter will serve the purpose.

- We've mentioned that radio does much of its business with commuters. Prime time is six to nine A.M. and three to seven P.M. A prime-time interview in even the smallest radio station is probably worth more than a public-affairs slot in all but the largest television markets. In some markets such as Los Angeles, where people rely heavily on automobile transportation, publicists open the champagne when they get a drive-time radio booking on a 50,000-watt station.

FM STATIONS

AM stands for ampitude modulation, and FM stands for frequency modulation, a mode of transmission that produces a

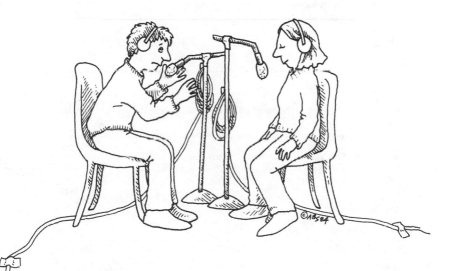

At the beginning of a radio interview, an engineer will adjust your
voice level to match the volume of your interviewer's. Be careful to
avoid bobbing and weaving around the microphone, raising or lowering your voice abruptly, or pounding the table for emphasis. Even
though the atmosphere is far more relaxed than on television, you're
still "on" in public.

signal far less prone to interference and static. Unless you've been in Samoa for the past twenty years, you may have noticed that FM has grown up to become radio's dominating music medium. Frequency and power considerations are less important to the publicity seeker than is the case on AM.

FM programmers often prefer a "short form" interview, meaning a sixty- or ninety-second feature rotated to various slots throughout the broadcast day. Don't feel slighted if the interviewer spends only fifteen minutes with you. The interview may be heard by more people than you ever imagined.

Ask about the station's "format," that is, what kind of music it plays and for whom. Music stations, be they AM or FM, use a form of shorthand to define format. If someone says to you, "We used to be MOR, now we're AOR, but I really think adult contemp is where it's at," he means that the radio station once played middle-of-the-road adult music, then switched to album-oriented rock, but should consider moving in the direction of hit records that appeal to people old enough to vote. When you hear that kind of alphabet soup, redirect your question to a station's *demographics.* It's all but impossible to make jargon out of descriptions as straightforward as "adults twenty-five to forty-nine."

RADIO RATINGS

If you visit three stations in a market and each visit leaves you with the impression that you've been to the "#1!!!" station in the city, you'll get an idea of the radio ratings game. Ratings, as compiled by Arbitron and other sources, are carefully measured, clearly reported, and loosely translated. There is but one #1 in any given ratings sweep. The confusion lies with the demographics. "*We're* number one in young adults. *We're* number one in news. *We're* number one in ethnic programming. But *we* are number one overall!" Overall would be considered the reigning champ. Make it easy on yourself by asking how many listeners there are in the time slot or "day part" when your interview will air.

Radio is your best media pal and should be regarded with the lifelong affection we reserve for a few special friends. It will always be there for you.

15
Television Interviews

Television is no longer an adequate term to describe the pyrotechnics of modern video. Your television screen will soon enable you to shop, bank, study, invest in the market, protect your home, make an airline reservation, view an athletic event, see a movie in 3-D without glasses, conduct a meeting with someone half a world away, send mail, and, for all we know, order a test-tube baby. Preparing for television is one of life's necessities because, like it or not, we're all going on the tube.

Ironically, television's evolution into narrowly targeted audiences brings it closer in mission to the radio it superseded nearly forty years ago. With the capacity to receive more than a hundred channels and the likelihood of expansion to as many viewing sources as a free market economy will allow, we now have a video spectrum so complex that our viewing guides could become as thick as our telephone directories. Here's a brief course on what you're getting into:

Television. The term *television* refers to the over-air transmission of broadcast signals that are advertiser- or foundation-financed and available to viewers at no charge. In other words, the same VHF and UHF TV that has influenced our culture since the early fifties.

Cable. In 1948, a Pennsylvania appliance dealer named John Walson couldn't sell anyone in his town a television set because the Blue Mountains impeded the reception of signals. Walson climbed to the top of the highest peak and, using army surplus wire strung through trees, he rigged an antenna. Anyone who bought a set was offered a free hookup. In his attempt to sell a few Philcos, Walson joined the ranks of Alexander Graham Bell, Samuel F.B. Morse, and Guglielmo Marconi. He invented the field of cable television.

For decades, cable subsisted as a television-antenna service that served rural areas where reception was weak. Local operators threw in some weather, news, or high school sports coverage to spice up the offering. In the mid-sixties, cable began to weave its way through the streets of New York and other large cities. Skeptics doubted that it would last in these areas and were almost proven right. Cable operators found the municipal bureaucracies and wiring expenses far more difficult to overcome than they had anticipated. But the lure of static-free signals, distant stations, more sports coverage, and, finally, satellite-delivered cable networks proved irresistible.

Basic Cable Versus Pay Cable. On September 30, 1975, Time-Life, Inc., fired the starting gun of today's video revolution by taking their commercial-free movie service, Home Box Office, sending its signal to RCA's Satcom I satellite, and bringing it back to earth for distribution by cable systems. This event produced in cable a mitotic division into basic and pay-cable services.

Basic cable is today's version of the antenna service. You pay the cable company a monthly fee and they deliver clear reception of local channels, out-of-town television stations, and a selection of advertiser-supported cable-programming services such as Cable News Network. For an additional monthly charge, you are offered commercial-free networks such as

The set of a television talk show can produce disorientation and panic for an interviewee. Look only at your interviewer and force yourself to keep your focus on the conversation. Eventually, you'll scarcely notice the crew when you're on the air.

HBO. These networks are supported by the fees you pay and are known as pay-cable networks.

Subscription Television (STV). In areas where cable is not available, broadcast stations scramble their signals and offer programming similar to cable networks to subscribers who pay a monthly fee, usually higher than that for cable services. The programming source rents decoders that unscramble the signal. This form of television is also known, simply, as pay TV.

Low-Power Television (LPTV). In the early eighties, the Federal Communications Commission was in a mood of deregulation that reflected the overall philosophy of the Reagan administration. In this spirit, the commission authorized the broadcast of local programming on low-power television translators, which have been traditionally used to bolster the range of television stations. The action gives rise to the tantalizing possibility of up to 8,000 mom-and-pop television stations available to interview you or broadcast your videotape by 1990. Many feel that LPTV will never survive on that scale, but one must remember the fifties and sixties when the same skeptics believed that anyone attempting to proliferate cable programming would die of malnutrition.

Multipoint Distribution Service (MDS). A method of video transmission that uses microwave signals to broadcast programming, data text, or other services to subscribers, MDS is of interest to professionals and educators as well as pay services who sell programming to hotels, apartment buildings, and, to a lesser extent, private households. Whether MDS proliferates or drowns in the cascade of video options is an open question. Our guess is that you will use it one day to publicize products or ideas of a technical or esoteric nature.

Instructional Television Fixed Service (ITFS). This is the PBS of MDS—microwave transmission allocated solely for the use of nonprofit organizations. The Catholic Church makes extensive use of ITFS channels for its parochial schools.

Direct Broadcast Satellites (DBS). In 1982, a new generation of high-powered satellites that will make it possible for programmers to transmit directly to homes equipped with low-cost receiving dishes was authorized by the FCC. Many believe that DBS technology will ultimately replace cable, but that is far from being resolved. We know that DBS will offer you many more opportunities to appear on the air.

Satellite Master Antenna Television (SMATV). This rapidly proliferating field is essentially cable television on private property such as apartment buildings, condominium complexes, mobile home parks, and office buildings. Part of SMATV's appeal is its freedom from regulation. There are no local politicians involved in its franchising, and systems are generally exempted from the FCC's definition of a cable system. You are in a strong position to publicize to a homogeneous audience when you are interviewed on, or submit a videotape to, an SMATV system.

High-Definition Television (HDTV). Since the 1939 World's Fair, we've lived with a television picture consisting of 525 video lines that scan the screen. The Japanese Broadcasting Corporation has developed a comparative utopia with 1,125 lines that offer superior color fidelity, sharper pictures, and stereo sound. HDTV will probably boost the advancement of DBS as it needs too much band space to offer a feasible conversion of our UHF and VHF systems.

Teletext. Teletext is an electronic publishing service that gives a user access to an unlimited variety of information such as news, sports, airline schedules, market quotes, and classified advertisements.

Videotex.   Videotex is the two-way version of teletext, where a user dials a number and conducts transactions with the information received. Banks are especially interested in videotex, but the possibilities are unlimited. It does not take Picasso's imagination to realize the potential for publicity in those data banks.

Closed-Circuit Television (CCTV).   Closed-circuit television, also known as nonbroadcast video, is a global term referring to all television pictures that are not transmitted. Schools, hospitals, offices, and just about any locale where people work are brimming with videotape recorders and cameras. The proliferation of tape libraries is something every publicity-conscious individual should watch

THE CREW

The above are the *modes* of video under which flow channels, subchannels, subsubchannels, networks, subnetworks, subsubnetworks, and programming sources into infinity. If you ever harbored any idea about escaping to a Pacific island to avoid the complexities of civilization, now's the time to buy your ticket. Otherwise, prepare to go on television. Meet your crew.

In the control room, you'll find a director who wears headphones and faces a wall of monitors. Her job is to keep the production under control by telling everyone what to do. The rest of the crew, you'll notice, also wears headphones. Also in the control room are an associate director, an audio operator to make sure the microphone on your lapel doesn't distort your voice, a technical director to keep everything, especially video integrity of the picture, humming smoothly, a graphics operator to summon a show's titles and logos, and any number of videotape operators. A local cable production might have a single person performing these functions; a network telecast will have more.

On the studio floor are camera operators, a floor director, one or more electronics technicians, lighting specialists, a makeup artist, segment producers, associate producers, "gofers" (who go-fer coffee or paper clips), station personnel, and other functionaries who can make your first video interview as terrifying as hanging over the side of the Grand Canyon by a ribbon. Be prepared to see these people and, for the first few television experiences, remind yourself that they'll be there. Eventually they'll cease to be scary.

The crew will often be indifferent to you, and who can blame them? They do this every day. In a major market, even the sorriest talk show gets celebrities who prowl the publicity circuit. You are today's fresh pastry, interesting but not especially unusual. Before air time be prepared for private little jokes that might include you without your awareness as the camera operator focuses on one of your freckles. They love it when a man's fly is unzipped. They have to zoom in and out to focus before going on the air, so why not do an extreme closeup of a half-mast zipper? Don't worry, you won't go on that way. Some devastatingly attractive twenty-two-year-old woman from the production staff will whisper in your ear and make you wish you had drowned as a child. Do yourself a favor and avoid all this. Check yourself out thoroughly before you get to the set.

For the most part, the crew just comes to work and performs in a calm, professional manner. It would be a bad idea to judge their reaction, or lack of it, to your interview. Occasionally, a technician will inform you that you were fascinating, or that he was moved to tears. Not to be cynical, but this one is moved to tears three or four times weekly.

It should also come as no surprise if your interviewer has little to say to you off-camera. He or she may be apprehensive about chitchat for fear of diluting energy, a very real superstition based on hard experience. A staffer may ask for your visuals and, if you don't have any, groan, "Oh God! Talking heads!" or some other flattering remark. You will note then, if you had not done so before, that sensitivity is not a requisite for a job in broadcasting.

A television environment has more ritual than a Cape Canaveral launch. Hand signals fly. Cue cards and teleprompters appear as monitors are wheeled in. You might hear someone say, "Quiet on the set," as very hot lights come on and start to bake you. No one has told you where to look, and you wonder in a panic if you're supposed to direct your attention toward the camera or your interviewer.

Don't worry about anything but your now-rehearsed act. Sit up straight but don't be rigid, and look only toward your interviewer. Stand by to be interrupted, for television differs dramatically from radio in the pace and momentum of its interviews. Your host's job depends on providing a very quick pace. Ten- to thirty-second responses to questions are the norm here.

VISUALS

It's perfectly all right if you don't have a set of supplementary visual aids during a television interview. If you do, however, you'll probably have an asset. Is there anything you can physically carry to a television interview that will assist in your interview presentation? If not, is there anything you can put on videotape? If your company has ¾" video equipment, you may be able to shoot a short demonstration tape of your product. Otherwise, check the phone book under "video" and you'll be able to find an inexpensive video facility that can shoot a tape for you. If you bring in a demo tape on Beta or VHS, the quality may not be acceptable to the program.

Photographs should be mounted on a background of thin but

firm blue or black cardboard. You might find 35mm slides, also acceptable in most studios, more convenient.

To save a frantic moment before the show, carry an index card with your name on one line and your company or product on the line below. This may not be necessary, but if a member of the crew asks for it, just hand over the card and be assured that your pitch is being flashed beneath your head as you speak.

THE REMOTE INTERVIEW

A very common publicity experience is the remote interview: a reporter and crew arrive at the house or office and shoot for an interval that ranges between thirty minutes and several hours.

Give them something to see. If your office is less appealing than an outdoor garden, take the crew outside, weather permitting. If there are especially interesting visuals that can be intercut with your conversation, be sure to point them out. The crew is there to break up the tedium of the studio. Help them out.

Be careful of what you say in a remote interview. All of your great pearls of wisdom will be compressed into a short feature or inserted into a story with a broader scope. The responses that you feel give the opportunity for "great copy" may come back to haunt you when the editing is done.

Feed the crew. Have coffee and pastry available. The interviewer has to avoid fattening indulgences, but the lighting and camera people sometimes endure hours of jumping in and out of a van. They'll make you look good if they're happy with you.

If you're running a company that demands your time and the crew would like to take four or five hours away from the day, you need not feel compelled to accommodate such a request. Be polite but excuse yourself.

KISS ME AGAIN

Constantly put your repertoire of question responses through the strainer so that you're prepared for the cardinal rule of television conversation, brevity. Any question that can't be answered within the medium's ten- to thirty-second attention span hasn't been properly reworked. If you have many thoughts and subparagraphs to your material (and you should have enough, remember, to talk for fifteen minutes without interruption), you can always keep coming back toward your main point.

Television is far more focused on who you are than on what you have to say. Long after your text is forgotten, your image will be remembered if you are effective. Don't worry if you didn't get to say enough. In publicity, there's always tomorrow.

16
Print Interviews

Radio's cultural impact rests with its music. Its scandals tend to be lurid accounts of disc jockeys and other station personnel being bribed with money, sex, or drugs. Television has the clout and gets corrupted in every possible manner—quiz-show scandals, union problems, and the old standbys of money, drugs, and sex. For a long time the print media functioned well in their role as society's referee. Things changed in the early eighties.

Maybe we expected too much of print, especially after two young reporters unearthed Watergate. There are a thousand dimestore analyses of what did happen, but, fundamentally, newspapers got caught up in a scoop mentality as they fought against waning circulations and advertising, and stepped-up competition from television. A few reporters got careless.

Despite the controversies and excesses that involve a sparse minority of reporters and editors, print remains a credible news source and probably the most effective publicity outlet available to you. When you and your picture appear in the newspaper, or in a regional magazine, people remember it for a long time. They clip it, file it, take it out years later and remind you of what you said. In print, you have a credibility that carries its own mystique. Print is probably also the only medium that will come close to covering your full story.

Don't be surprised if your interviewer is more guarded than she or he would have been a few years ago. The problems came when editors trusted their reporters completely and were betrayed. That trust remains print's cornerstone, but the checks and balances within the newsroom have changed. Expect to be challenged on your statistics, and, if it's a little fantastic, your background.

The print interview is unique in its interpretive nature. Someone will be writing about you, describing your office or den, talking about your children, and quoting you. You'll say a lot and be quoted a little. Be sure that you speak to a reporter in language that accurately reflects the image you wish to convey.

Say: "I think the world has too many defective widgets."

Don't say: "A lot of morons are glutting the market with their junky widgets."

If you were the writer of a widget article, which quote would you use? What choice would you have? If an executive calls his competitors morons, you're certainly not going to go for the tamer quote. You might even want to encourage this spiciness by asking your subject if he would venture to name any of those morons.

"Let me go on the record as saying that there hasn't been an IQ of over seventy-five at Walden Widget since World War II."

Now if you were the reporter, your heart would be pounding through your vest pocket. You would certainly not wish the subject of your interview to restrict the flow of his words. It is not a reporter's job to do that. You might even press forward.

"I gather then that you are saying that the president of Walden Widget lacks intelligence."

"I'm saying that the president of Walden Widget is a moron."

There is only one moron in this transaction. If the whole hypothetical case sounds farfetched, and if you believe that a person smart enough to be a corporation president is too smart to make such remarks, you are mistaken. People who are otherwise brilliant make phenomenal blunders with reporters, especially in print where there's no technology to keep us in check. In a situation such as this, a good reporter would encourage a sense of bravado. The headline: WIDGET PREZ CALLS COMPETITORS "MORONS."

"But I thought it was off the record! I'm ruined!" says the ruined widget president. To finish this scenario, the next edition of the newspaper (or the same issue) would carry a photograph of Walden's chief executive officer next to his Harvard alumnus chair, while the company psychologist would be quoted as saying that Walden personnel are "above the norm" in intelligence. The interview subject would be playing the guitar for pocket change before the end of the week.

Once you make a negative public impression, you're stuck with it regardless of update stories or retractions. You don't have to guard every word, but bear in mind that a reporter does not owe you any explanation for the tone of his article. Treat a reporter as you would treat a live microphone.

The positive side of the equation comes with the length of the feature. In print, you can express yourself without the constant interruptions of radio and television. And there is no reason to assume that the reporter is out to get you. There is a bundle of nice news published every day, and you're probably going to be part of it.

A good journalist will make you want to talk about interesting things, and you must be sure that those interesting things are in your best interest. Know your act and glide from one topic to the other as you would in any environment. If you're drinking, either limit yourself to a single drink or stay away from alcohol altogether. If something is "off the record," be sure that you specify that and that the tape recorder goes off. If you don't trust the reporter, don't say anything off the record. It's that simple.

If you are dealing with extraordinarily sensitive material, some of which is on and some of which is off the record, tape the interview yourself. You're under no obligation to confess if your interviewer fails to probe. Sometimes they don't even want to. A feature writer for the "Life-style" section probably isn't looking to roast you on your own backyard grill.

There is also the possibility of inaccuracy. Part of that is the human nature of interpretation, and part of it is that issues are not always as ice-water clear as you intended them to be in your discussion. If it's important, repeat it, pause for emphasis, and approach the conversation with the showmanship you use in television.

Know your good side if a photographer accompanies the reporter. Sometimes the pictures will be taken at a later date, either at the newspaper itself where the lighting is right or at your most photogenic location.

Visuals are as important in print as they are in television. A photograph dramatically increases the value of a feature.

If your interviewer is a columnist, be familiar with his or her work well in advance of the interview. If the column is gossipy, ask if you can submit items at a later date. You will be amazed at the power of this kind of relationship.

It may take a while for the publication to run your piece. Be polite in inquiring if the article has been scheduled, but don't be a nuisance. If it doesn't run at all, and that happens periodically, don't blame yourself. Sometimes editors rule out features because they resemble recent stories, or because someone just didn't like the flow of the writing.

When the article does appear, the whole process will have been worth it. In addition to print's bestowing credibility, nothing generates more publicity than a good clipping. At the very least, your family will be proud.

17
Controlling the Interview

Your interviewers have an obligation to keep from turning your conversation into yet another commercial on an oversold show. Some will plug your pitch harder than others. It's up to you to strike a balance between where you want the interview to go and where the interviewer wants to take it.

Interviewers are happiest when it's going well. If you shine most brightly when discussing the topics most conducive to your plug and place less emphasis in areas of conversation that interest you less, you'll have a lot more input into the course of the interview. Let us illustrate with a hypothetical case.

After finding that your exercise and diet program works, you put together a small book that the major publishers decline. They do so on the basis of two criteria: They have large inventories of their own yet-to-be-published books that are similar in format, and they are candid enough to tell you that books of this nature sell best when they are written either by a medical doctor or by a well-known personality. You are neither.

Undaunted, you find a printer, publish your own booklet, and hit the road for its publicity. Let's look in on one of your interviews:

"I'm Les Martel with Cindy Barbour, author of a new book called *Be Thin Next Month*, a thirty-day diet and exercise program that she says will give any overweight person a fresh start in the short space of a month. Welcome to *Good Morning Charlestown*. Why did you decide to write this book?"

(Naturally, you've anticipated this question and have prepared an answer that gives you the opportunity to take the reins.)

"Well, Les, the book comes as a result of my own experience when I took off twenty pounds in thirty days and kept it off. You see, there are thousands of diet and exercise programs, but very few work because they lack one basic element . . ."

(Does old Les really have a big choice about what he can ask after your pause?)

"What's that?"
"A personal contract with one's self, Les. I've found plenty of books, and they're all effective enough, but I've never found one with a personal contract. That's where my book begins. In fact, I have what I think is a unique offer to readers."
"Tell me about it."
"I offer a box of their favorite chocolates plus a full refund if they choose not to advance beyond page three of *Be Thin Next Month*. I consider page three to be the most critical page because the plan can't proceed without it."
"Let me read aloud from page three of *Be Thin Next Month*, Cindy."

Many people fall into the trap of believing they're selling their product by continuous repetition of its name.

"Well, Les, in my book, *Be Thin Next Month* . . ."
"In *Be Thin Next Month*, I say . . ."
"Before I wrote *Be Thin Next Month* . . ."

A limited amount of such hype is permissible, but Les has options, too:

"Frankly, Cindy, I wish you wouldn't mention the title so much, because I'm not sure of its validity. You're not a doctor, and you're putting out a diet."

Or,

"Cindy, I want to thank you but we're out of time."

Your host can always run out of time and extend the next interview segment. If it's a live interview where there are no other guests, there's always the phone. Anyone who interviews daily knows how to get tough. The sweet ones enjoy the change, and the tough talkers simply return to a natural conversational habit. Either way, you're in for a bad time if you oversell. Suppose, though, that you've taken the time to come all the way to a studio and there has been no plug. Then it's up to you to slip one in:

"That's all the time we have, Cindy. Thanks for showing us those great exercises."
"My pleasure, Les. I'd like to remind people that all those exercises can be found in my new book, *Be Thin Next Month*, on special this month at all Pen & Ink bookstores in the greater Charlestown area."

In most cases, the plugs will come at the beginning and end of a broadcast interview with titles appearing under your name as you speak to the television audience. That's why you have been advised to carry a typed index card to any TV appearance.

Suppose that the two questions you dread most come up anyway. If they're obvious to you, they're probably equally apparent to your interviewer:

> "Now, with all due respect, Cindy, you're not a doctor, and I must confess to a philosophical objection to laypeople with diet books. I have to tell our viewers to beware of *Be Thin Next Month*. I hope you can understand why."

And,

> "I understand that seven major publishers have turned this book down. So, I must ask you, why should we trust it?"

The press always gets an honest answer, or extracts a severe penalty from those who lie. The first step in controlling an interview is to prepare your case, its selling points, and its legitimacy before going under the lights. There are a number of ways to do that in the example of the diet book. Cindy could have had a physician consult on the book and write the foreword, ask the family doctor to endorse it, or solicit the advice and endorsement of a legitimate professional society.

> "I agree, Les, and that's why the foreword of the book was written by Dr. Perry Foster, who is on the staff of St. Luke's hospital here in Charlestown."

(If she takes a brief pause here, she ends this line of questioning and moves quickly to her next thought.)

". . . which reminds me, Les . . . when we were going
through the exercise portion of the book, I asked Dr. Foster about the efficiency of sit-ups, and he said . . ."

Or, suppose there was no Dr. Foster in the preparation of
her book. She realizes she should have thought of a medical endorsement, but it's too late now.

"While it's true that I don't have a medical degree, I'm
sure that any M.D. in practice would not take issue with
the menus, which were prepared in accordance with published standards of the American Dietary Association, or
the exercises, which have been used for years. In fact, I
advise all my readers to see a doctor before undertaking
any diet or exercise program."

Here, the author is falling back on a second line of legitimacy. When you check your own pitch, you'll always be able
to find something that makes sense, or you wouldn't have come
on the show in the first place. The key is to know ahead of time
what's going to occur and, if you are surprised, to take a beat
and not panic.

As for the question of Cindy's book having been rejected by
major publishers, the truth wouldn't be a bad idea:

"Seven publishers turning down a book is a rather common experience for even the most seasoned authors.
I was not discouraged by the publishers but was told
that they had plenty of diet books. Besides, Les, the
most successful diet books are written by either famous
personalities or physicians. I'm neither, but I did take
off twenty pounds in thirty days, dozens of people I
know have had similar successes, and I know my plan
works."

The key principle of controlling an interview is *emphasis*. Be direct, never evasive, and always introduce the next topic yourself if the conversation is in an area where you are not comfortable.

DEVELOPING TRANSITIONS

Since controlling an interview is a matter of emphasizing areas of conversation, it's a good idea to develop and practice the conversational transitions that make change possible. Here are a few suggestions:

"You mentioned rainfall before, and it reminds me . . ."

(The "you mentioned" transition is always good once per interview because it unifies your thought with something the host said earlier.)

"That reminds me . . ."

"Have you ever found yourself in this situation, Les? You're walking down the street and suddenly . . ."

"One thing you should know about . . ."

(You can initiate a new topic—anything. There's no need to wait for an invitation.)

Always let the interviewer do the plug. If that doesn't happen:

"At Phoenix Widget, we believe . . ."

"The first time I saw one of these Phoenix five-hundreds, I thought it was a shovel."

"I'll bet you didn't know that this widget has more than three hundred uses."

* * *

You'll never be—and shouldn't be—in absolute control of your interview, but through directness, a positive approach, the establishment of legitimacy, and a determination to take charge without being pushy, you'll be in a much more comfortable, and much more productive, position in your new role as interviewee.

18
Adverse Publicity

It usually starts with a single call, perhaps when you're at home and not insulated by the protective machinery of an office staff. The reporter is friendly but direct. There is a document with your signature linking you to some dreadful group, event, fraud, or other criminal activity. Sometimes it's about someone you love, or a close associate. So begins your time when the press becomes more terrifying than the worst nightmare in your memory.

Adverse publicity requires a constant vigilance, a stamina beyond your finest athletic accomplishments. Life as you know it ends for the duration of the crisis; every hour of every day passes as painfully as the slow throb of an infected tooth. Reporters may camp in your neighborhood, interrupt you at church, interview coworkers and employees, and relentlessly pursue the truth you would rather not tell them. You may find yourself the innocent victim of an investigation that destroys your career.

Those who have endured the hot end of investigative journalism remain affected by the experience for the rest of their lives. One wrong move and you're imprinted in an unfavorable manner. There is no escape from the press, but there are ways in which you can survive the experience to your best advantage. We offer hypothetical cases for both the innocent and the guilty, beginning with the former.

YOU DIDN'T DO IT

A very human response is to go public immediately and nip the problem in the bud. If the reporter has called you, however, it is likely that erroneous circumstantial evidence has implicated you enough to warrant a thorough examination before rendering any statement. It is also possible that a party whose identity is unknown to you at this time is attempting to deflect culpability by accusing you.

The reporter may use pressure. There's a deadline, so-and-so says you authorized the misappropriation of funds, and if you refuse comment, he'll have no choice but to print that. It won't look very good for you. There's nothing wrong (even though you may be made to feel otherwise) with a simple assertion of your innocence and a refusal to comment further until you have had the opportunity to examine the evidence. Leave it at that and get an attorney.

Your lawyer should be a fighter who isn't afraid to stand firm with reporters. Some hotshots see any publicity as a bonanza to be used in a later race for public office. Beware of this type, although many competent attorneys seek election. Once you choose an attorney, you'll have to make a few fast decisions.

The Statement. If you're directly accused of wrongdoing, you may want to draft a statement that will ward off such damaging comments as:

Neither Mr. Sherwood nor his attorney, Robert Cohen, returned numerous calls made to their offices on Tuesday.

Or,

> While Sherwood has refused to comment, sources inside North American Lumber report that the executive has not been seen since reports of his alleged misconduct surfaced last Monday.

You may prefer instead to issue a formal comment such as:

> My attorney, Mr. Cohen, and I have conferred with the District Attorney's office and disclosed as much information as we have available. I am confident that this matter will be resolved through proper legal channels. I wish to state unequivocally that I have done nothing illegal or unethical with regard to this matter.

Now there's something to print. It says little, but it says *something.* When the questions accelerate, you might add the following verbal remark:

> I have been advised by my attorney that any further comment would be inappropriate at this time.

The Firm Disclaimer. In some cases, a direct response to specific allegations *is* the best course. Make sure that your attorney reviews your case with you and participates in your decision. Then, be prepared to stand calm during some very tough questioning. Start with a prepared statement that you'll immediately make available in the form of a written release. Be as specific as circumstances and your lawyer's advice permit.

Never lie. Once you get caught in any kind of misstatement, you're going to be in a vulnerable position for the duration of the crisis. Once you firmly deny your story, make yourself available to as many interviewers as you can handle.

The Total Silence. If you refuse to say anything at all—
nothing—you can never be misquoted or quoted out of context. If you choose this difficult course, we recommend that
you say nothing at all instead of the terse "No comment" that
comes across as evasive. Total silence, as is the case with other
courses, should be undertaken only on the advice of at least one
attorney.

The Single Interview. Sometimes you trust a reporter and want
to share your story with him or her. This path is flooded with
the danger of mistreatment and relentless hounding by competing publications or stations. But if it's a comprehensive account, thoroughly documented and verified in every way
possible, it can also send the pack to their next story.

YOU DID IT

You have all of the options of the innocent with the addition
of more vulnerability during the earliest stages of the crisis.
You can say things that you'll later regret but won't be able to
take back. You also have the joint dilemma of coconspirators,
if there are any, talking to the press while your own attorney
advises you to keep silent.

Admit your guilt to yourself and build a worst-case scenario,
enumerating with your lawyer all of the facts that could come
out in the investigation. Reporters make friends quickly, and
they're not going to be shy about using whatever tactic is necessary to get their story.

If you can develop the presence to regard the press with the
professional wariness of any adversary relationship, you're less
likely to lose control. Don't try to win them over and don't try
to scare them away.

The "don't lie" rule applies more rigorously than ever when
you're guilty. Don't even tell a fib. But you're under no obligation to confess either, for you are innocent until a court of law

says otherwise. Don't try to fan the publicity flames hoping that the negative exposure will get your case thrown out of court. It usually doesn't work.

Be strong and professional. Don't be goaded because a mob accosts you with lights, microphones, and cameras. Don't throw your coat over your head like some street mugger caught snatching a purse. As difficult as this may be, act as though they're not there.

"The best defense is a good offense," you may say as you start coming on strong. Sometimes that works, but it works a lot better for the innocent. If there's solid evidence adding up, you're going to look awfully silly for having roared.

Don't give up. Your story is as perishable as grapefruit in a supermarket. Eventually the clamor will die down and people's memories will dim. They're likely to remember more about your presence than the facts in the case itself. If you remain publicly sincere and courageous, you will be remembered that way by many. If you twitch, wail, hide, or clam up, the damage will linger. Eventually, though, you will become a stale piece of news. And that's the best news of all.

19
The Tour Circuit

It's three A.M., and you wake up in a panic. You don't know where you are, and, for an instant, you're not even sure who you are. The surroundings of the room tell you nothing except that you're in a hotel and it's indistinguishable from where you have spent the last ten nights. Then it becomes clear. You're on tour in Columbus. Or is it Cincinnati? Right, Cincinnati. Columbus was yesterday. Wasn't it?

A tour is an efficient and economical promotional mechanism that enables anyone to saturate the nation through local media exposure. If a tour doesn't move what you're selling, nothing will.

Before attempting the rigors of touring, there are a number of items to keep in mind:

Is there enough money? A tour may be efficient, but the costs are not measured in coins. Air travel generally occurs during peak flying hours, hotels in major cities top a hundred dollars a day for even modest accommodations, and the long-distance calls add up.

Is there enough time? The biggest mistake made by novice tour publicists is not allowing for the lead time of most television shows. Your material should be in a producer's hands four to six weeks prior to your arrival in a city. You'll need to factor in the number of missed telephone connections with production people, and the amount of time you'll spend on hold before getting a booking. A healthy ten-city tour has fifty to seventy-five bookings that come as the result of hundreds of calls.

Is there enough product distribution to warrant the time and expense? There's no point in going anywhere if a city's market for your pitch is not clearly anticipated and well stocked.

Have you enough in the budget to spend a few hundred for the proper reference materials and perhaps even a professional consultation? A common experience at PR firms begins with someone walking in the front door with a great idea. He'll book the smaller cities, and all the firm has to do is take care of New York, Chicago, Los Angeles, and the national shows. The "client" is then shocked to learn either that his money is declined or that there is virtually no difference in price between this "cinch" assignment and a full-blown campaign.

More information on national media appears in Chapter 25. In the case of large markets such as New York, Chicago, and Los Angeles, no one has an easy time booking cities where producers routinely choose between Henry Kissinger, Sylvester Stallone, and Harry from Phoenix Widget. As in any business, PR firms charge according to the expenditure of time and personnel. Knowing something about these realities should help you prepare to deal with a professional publicity firm. Perhaps you'll find that a professional consultation is well within your budget after all.

You may want to hire either a free-lance publicist or a capable person to make the phone calls. In tour publicity, it is not possible to be away from the calls once the booking begins.

All of Chapter 9's booking rules apply to the making of a tour, with the added factor of *momentum.* Once you set cities and dates, you are locked into a mail/overnight express/phone/scheduling pattern that will topple the tour in domino fashion if the pace falters. You will experience intense aggravation. You don't have to accept the tour's challenges to your mental health—insults, changes in schedule, last-minute cancellations, hotel hassles, airline blunders, indifference, and rudeness—as permanent in your life, but for the six or eight weeks of your tour involvement, you would do well to brace for frustration.

PRE-TOUR PLANNING

First, choose your cities. You need to learn something about the demographic content of each city you visit along with getting a thumbnail notion of its local media picture. If you're selling snowmobiles, you wouldn't go to San Diego. That one is obvious. But if you're using a rodeo to sell alcoholic beverages, or an athletic event to sell cigarettes, there are areas of the country where you will be unwelcome. Having chosen your cities, sit down with an atlas and line them up geographically:

Boston	Minneapolis/St. Paul
New York	Denver
Philadelphia	Los Angeles
Pittsburgh	San Francisco
Cleveland	Portland
Detroit	Seattle
Chicago	

Take your cities to a travel agent and try to work out the most economical package available. Price wars and deregulation notwithstanding, you probably won't benefit from any "supersaver" rates on the short hauls of a promotional tour. Generally, you don't need more than one day in each city.

TIME	SHOW & STATION	PLACE	CONTACT	COMMENTS
8:45 AM	Good Morning Springfield WSJB-TV	WSJB-TV 2613 No. Dorette (Near Dobson Lake Rd.)	Peter Pellenz (208) 427-2265	Live out by 10:00
10:30 AM	The Mike Noyes Show WBUG Radio	23 Dobson Lake Rd. (three blocks from WSJB-TV)	Mike Noyes (208) 377-4770	Live with call-ins until noon.
1:15 PM	Press Interview Lunch with Sandy Booth, Lifestyle Editor, THE SPRINGFIELD TIMES	The China Dragon Route 3, Horseff	Sandy Booth (208) 427-1172	Ms. Booth will meet you at restaurant
2:30 PM	"Perspective" WTEL Radio	Communications Center South Third Floor	Ellen Harris (208) 890-0909	Taping out by 3:15
4:45 PM	Springfield At Five WSTV-TV	WSTV Studios 2435 Senecaline	John Persons (208) 429-9227	Live Newscast out by 6:00

The Booking Grid. Always use one grid page for each city and make notations in pencil.

THE BOOKING GRID

There is a lot of information to keep on hand during the several weeks you'll need to book a tour. Page 155 will introduce you to the most efficient manner of keeping this information in one place, the booking grid. Use one grid page for each city and make notations in pencil. Unless you have already proved yourself to be extraordinarily strong in enduring interviews, it is recommended that you spend no more than two weeks on the road during your first tour. If you wish to continue, book another leg.

Now that your grids are stapled and lined up in geographic order, assign dates to each city. Remember, one date to each city and don't book any cities for Saturdays or Sundays unless you have a special event planned that will warrant weekend publicity.

Scan your reference material and take careful notes on what you consider the best shows in each city. Don't write them on a grid but make pencil markings within the reference text itself. Public-affairs interviews and public-access cable shows are wonderful for media training, but you're in a new league when you start touring. You want the best shows you can find.

Open any PR reference text (see Chapter 27) and look for television or radio programs that are on the air every day. Live shows are usually better than taped programs, but there are no ironclad rules. The references usually tell you where the 50,000-watt all-talk AM stations are, and you'll soon learn to pinpoint the morning talk shows that have the most consistently surveyed audiences. The references also give estimated audience figures. Make a list of your preferred bookings for each city. For example:

TOLEDO

AM Toledo, WTOL-TV: Betty Simon (318) 222-3300

The Denise Brisson Show, WDBS Radio: Peg Bailey (318) 490-1230

The Jerry Clarke Show, WRBJ Radio: Jerry Clarke (318) 791-4545

The Toledo Express:

Life-style: Gary Girard (318) 344-4676

"Around Toledo": Patty McMahon (318) 344-4658

"About Women": Marcel Dumont (318) 344-4692

Business: Bob Madden (318) 344-4625

Toledo Today, WDEV-TV: Kenny Foster (318) 791-8500

Impact, WJMR Radio: Chris Katz (318) 791-3300

Perspective, Toledo Cable: Carolyn Kristen (318) 344-2102

Dr. Jerome's Diary, WDPP Radio: Dr. Jerome Parnell (318) 344-2121

Toledo Magazine: Terry Daniel (318) 222-4444

Now you'll need to make a preliminary set of calls to meet the contacts and let them know that you're sending material on your topic and would they be interested? Not everyone does it this way. Some professionals never make a call without sending material, and others never send material until they've heard the word "yes." Since you don't know the contacts, a preliminary round of calls is highly recommended. Now get set for the first round of booking blues.

"I'll have to get back to you."

"I'm really busy right now."

"We're going on the air in two minutes."

"Too bad I didn't hear from you last week. We just did that topic last Thursday."

"We never do that topic."

"It sounds like the pits."

"Call me Friday."

"Send the materials and I'll look."

Don't count on the person who says, "Yes, that sounds really interesting," to even remember your call next week, let alone be interested. But keep plugging, stopping only for meals, and a pattern will start to emerge for each city. Sometimes you'll have to use Express Mail or a comparable overnight mail service. You won't like it, but time is everything once your cities and dates are set. Do not dwell on a single city as you book. If a major television program or newspaper fails to materialize in any city, skip it and rearrange. You don't want to endure the expense for a few taped radio interviews. Once the preliminary calls have established who in each city is or is not interested, do your mailings and make the follow-up calls. The following guidelines should help to assess your booking priorities for various types of interviews:

Morning television talk shows—book three to four weeks ahead of your arrival.

Live radio shows that appear on the air every day—book three to four weeks ahead of time.

Taped television interview programs—book about four weeks ahead of your scheduled arrival date.

Television news features—book extremely close to deadline, sometimes on the day of your arrival itself.

Newspaper press interviews—these all-important bookings sometimes can be booked a month ahead of time, and sometimes at the last minute.

Taped radio interviews—book about four weeks ahead of your arrival, but they can often be used to fill out a schedule near the last minute.

Local origination cable shows—book usually about three weeks ahead of time, sometimes at the last minute. Make certain that they've been on the air for a while before booking them. Sometimes these bookings are a total waste of time on tour.

TELEPHONE INTERVIEWS

A tour is not a vacation, and there's no reason to take the afternoon or the evening off. There are hundreds of radio stations, and small newspapers, dying to speak with you on the telephone. If you're not going to a particular city but wish exposure, check your references for stations or publications that offer telephone interviews.

CONFIRMING NOTES

Notes of confirmation are especially important when you're on the road. Be as specific as possible:

Mr. Peter Pellenz
Night Talk
WOR Radio
1440 Broadway
New York, NY 10018

Dear Mr. Pellenz:

It's a pleasure to confirm the appearance of Mr. Steve
Dworkin on WOR's Night Talk. Steve will arrive at the WOR
studios at 11:45 A.M. on Monday, June 22, for a live interview
at noon on the 24th floor of 1440 Broadway.

Please call me at (212) 345-6758 if there are any further
questions or information that might be helpful. I understand
Steve will be through at 1:00 P.M., but that you might want to
keep him for an extra half-hour for promotional
announcements. Thanks so much for your interest. I know it
will be a great interview.

Best,

John Rockwell

You may want to use only a preprinted postcard instead:

CONFIRMATION OF INTERVIEW

Guest:_____Steve Dworkin_____

Date:_____Monday, June 22_____

At:_____WOR, 1440 Broadway, 24th floor, 11:45 A.M.

Until:_____1:00 P.M. with possible taping until 1:30 P.M.

For further information, contact:_____John Rockwell,
(212) 345-6758

Any variation on the theme is appropriate. If possible, keep
copies of all confirmations with you on the road. You'll have

many experiences when you'll be glad you did. You'll also want copies of the travel agency's hotel confirmations lest you find yourself sleeping on a park bench because there's a convention in town and somehow the computer failed to register your impending arrival.

TYPING THE SCHEDULE

Once you leave home, your schedule will become something akin to a lifejacket. Careful typing of it is an imperative that is often overlooked by even the largest public relations agencies. Everything you need for a day of publicity should be typed on a *single page* and in order. Page 175 contains a sample of a typed tour schedule.

ON THE ROAD

While you're away, someone back at the office should have a copy of your schedule. That person should also reconfirm interviews and flights the day before your arrival in a city. If there is no one to do this for you, make time to do it yourself. The history of touring is littered with the bruised egos of people who endured the humiliating experience of having interviews canceled, showing up at the wrong place, or other horrors that can be avoided simply by calling a day ahead of time.

FOLLOWING UP

The same follow-up notes that you use in local publicity should be done when you come home from a tour. They always pay long-term dividends, even when you swear you'll never see your interview contacts again.

When you come home, you'll want to sleep for a month. You will have exhausted yourself and made mistakes. Some of the errors will make you want to cringe—you made a joke about bleached hair to a hostess with bleached hair, you showed up at the wrong time for a radio interview, or you rambled on about obesity when there was an overweight person on the talk-show panel. You may feel an uneasiness about what you actually accomplished. But you will know a secret. You will know how to do a tour, and, once you shower away the jet lag, you may even want to try it again.

20

Event
Publicity

The press has deserved some of its recent vilification. There have also, however, been an uncountable number of incidents where media people have gone beyond the boundaries of duty to help citizens in the most tragic of circumstances, medical emergencies.

In the emerging area of transplants, government appropriations sources have not kept pace with technology. The past several years have been witness to the most pathetic use of publicity imaginable. A man is told that he won't live unless a donor is found within the month. The medical center where the rare operation is to be performed cannot accommodate the patient unless he comes up with $75,000. There are also heart-wrenching stories of medical emergencies involving children, and the press goes way beyond the limits of ordinary coverage in attempts to locate young people who are kidnapped.

Event publicity is the gathering of exposure for a specific occurrence at a specific time. Whether your event is a yard sale or a rock concert, you will be called upon to work under intense deadline pressure with an ad hoc group of people who are often meeting for the first time.

Pledge drives for operations, marathons, sales of all kinds, and other mundane events receive a great deal of publicity when they are pegged to human need. Such effort is but a single facet of event publicity.

Usually events are publicized for more optimistic reasons. Sometimes, your church needs a roof or the town seeks a traffic light at a dangerous intersection. Perhaps you wish to rally people around a political issue you consider vital. Regardless of the cause's severity, there are certain dos and don'ts involved. There are also risks. The following pointers should help:

- Pick a type of event that no one is doing. If there have been three walkathons this spring, you'll have a difficult time garnering exposure.

- Choose the location as carefully as you would choose your own neighborhood. Can people get there? Will they want to go there?

- Everything takes longer than you think. Be generous in allocating time on the project.

- Pick a day when you're reasonably certain that a competing event will not occur. Parades, carnivals, and other public gatherings must obtain permission from the municipality. Check with City Hall.

- The more commercial the event, the more innovative it must be to warrant coverage. The press may be generous with worthy causes, but spectacles staged to sell soap have to offer a promise of novelty.

- Start way ahead of time in getting the required permissions from the community. You might be in a hurry, but they never are.

- Small towns work better than large cities. It's not impossible to get coverage in a city. People do it every day. But television crews are skeletal on weekends when most events occur, and your coverage potential will depend on the value of hard news made that day.

- Advance publicity is usually at least as important as coverage of the event itself. Again, start early.

- There is nothing quite as wonderful as a stunt that works, but stunts have a way of backfiring. You may find yourself hiding from the press instead of cultivating it if something goes wrong.

- The more dangerous the stunt, the more likely it is to get coverage. Need we remind you that you're going to get sued if someone gets hurt?

- Children, especially little ones, are always a big draw. They're also the most vulnerable to motion sickness and all kinds of danger, and they make a *lot* of noise.

The event follows a different pattern from booking guest shots. First, assess what you want to publicize and whether it ties in with any established date. There really *is* an Arbor Day. There is also a National Meat Week.

Next, get a release to all of the media and to the "Day Book" editors of the wire services. No matter where you live, you're not very far from a regional office of the Associated Press or United Press International. Call them and ask that your event be designated in the Day Book: a calendar of events checked daily by the subscribing media sources.

In addition to your release, there is a feature called "Community Calendar," "Town Crier," or some other similar name that is common to most radio or television stations. Take a 3" × 5" index card and type a couple of sentences about your event:

The women's auxiliary of American Legion Post 79 will sponsor a toy auction on Saturday, June 23, at the Bow Grange Hall from 10:00 A.M. to 6:00 P.M. Proceeds will benefit the Post 79 Scholarship Fund.

Then, stay on the phone as often as possible as the event draws near. Will the television station send a crew? Will the newspaper send a photographer? Keep on top of it until the very morning of the event.

Try to enlist the aid of local luminaries whose presence helps draw attention. They can always be put to work cutting ribbons, opening the festivities, receiving awards for their own community service, firing the starting gun of the race, or whatever. Part of the mayor's job is to put up with participation in worthy public events. Yours might as well be one of them. If there are voters present, most politicans will consider the event worthy. Local television people and disc jockeys will also sometimes be coaxed into helping with these tasks. In a sense, they're looking for votes, too.

Avoid planning an event that's too complicated. Costumed re-enactments of local historical occurrences are a good draw, but if they become too complex, you're apt to find yourself hosting a party that no one wants to attend.

There are many surprises in event publicity, the biggest of which is that sometimes the event is not publicized at all. When in doubt, see a public-relations consultant. You may find the fee a bargain. If you're planning a stunt of any kind, see an attorney, a public-relations consultant, and your Aunt Madeline who has great intuitive powers!

If you follow the guidelines, you'll live through it. The following suggestions can either be adapted in concept for your own event or may spawn other ideas:

Auction sales. People love the atmosphere of competitive bidding. Auctioneers usually work on a commission basis, and they work very fast. The combination of local dignitaries trying their skills as guest auctioneers and the jackhammer mouth of a professional works extremely well.

Anything that utilizes the talents of the very young or the very old. The press loves either extreme. As suggested earlier, these are our most fragile members of society, so be especially careful. Talent shows, contests, quizzes, and other mildly competitive events are a lot of fun.

Getting physical.   There seem to be two types of people in America—those who are fit and those who claim they'll one day stop procrastinating fitness. Either way, arm wrestling, running competitions, softball games, or anything that brings out the athletic fantasies in us will probably work if it hasn't been overdone in your community.

Used-merchandise sales.   People probably want to bargain more than they actually need so-called deals at used-merchandise sales. They don't draw much publicity unless there's an extraordinary angle, but not all events require much more than a brief announcement in the newspaper and on local stations.

Costumed events.   People love to dress up. The more people you persuade to dress in costumes, the more likely your possibility of coverage. Again, try and peg your costumed event to a particular day or point in history.

Animal events.   Animals always make good copy, especially if they're young and helpless. You can frequently find something a little more exotic than dogs and cats. In large cities, there are agencies that specialize in animals.

Demonstration.   On a more serious side of event publicity are demonstrations. They almost always draw press attention. Demonstrations are public gatherings and require the cooperation of public officials, some of whom may be the object of your protest. Reporters learned a long time ago to be wary of demonstrations staged for their own benefit rather than the public's. The outcome of a demonstration is rarely predictable, so, although they are your right as citizens, plan carefully to avoid regretting your decision.

21
The Press Conference

It's 10:30 A.M., and you've called a press conference for 11:00. The caterer has set up a folding table with an urn of coffee, doughnuts, pastries, and little sandwiches. There is a stage in the rented hotel banquet room and a lectern from which the president of your company will announce a merger. At the rear of the room are three tables for television camera operators to get the elevation they need.

You pace a bit, wondering if you've chosen the right-sized room. If there's too much unused space at a press conference, the momentum of the announcement is diminished. If the press is crowded into a room, there's a lot of discomfort. The president joins you.

"They did say they'd be here, didn't they?" he asks, and you assure him, for the fourth time this morning, that the press will come. They're always a little, er, late, ha ha. You ask the boss to go somewhere in the room because you don't want him greeting reporters as they come through the door. If they do. It's 10:45. Where the hell are they?

"Why do I have to leave? I'm not a movie star. I don't need a grand entrance," he says, in a way that questions your right to be in the human race.

"It's better, that's all." You know the boss is thinking that the press would be here by now if he'd brought in an outside consultant. He is incorrect.

What would be happening if you had brought in a public-relations firm is that you would have received another professional opinion on how to proceed with the merger's announcement. A press conference isn't always the solution.

At 10:51, the first member of the fourth estate, a reporter for *Widget Weekly*, arrives and heads for the refreshments.

"I'm starving," he says. "I knew you guys would have food. By the way, where is everybody?"

Freeze the action here and take a hard look at the situation. If the merger really is newsworthy, the press will soon arrive. If it isn't, you're going to humiliate yourself and maybe lose your job. Press conferences are not for the fainthearted. Perhaps you should have sent a series of personalized releases to each of the pertinent media people in your city. Keep the body identical but put the reporter's name at the top, send them by messenger, and stay by the phone to answer the inevitable questions. The boss's day would be interrupted by the calls requiring his involvement, but he wouldn't be pacing around the lobby of a Holiday Inn at this moment.

You stand convinced of your decision. This merger involves the livelihood of 500 employees, and you believe it's news. If the conference fails, you'll live with it, but you'll never be convinced that your instinct was incorrect. Sometimes, in dealing with the press, instinct is all we have.

Now let the action resume. Between 10:45 and 11:10, when the conference actually begins, a troop of reporters arrives. You receive a call from a television assignment editor who explains that the crew is just finishing a story nearby and will be right over. When everything is settled, you step up to the podium, tap the mike, adjust for squealing feedback, and start to speak.

"Ladies and gentlemen, it's my privilege to welcome you on

behalf of International Widget. Let me now introduce our president, Mr. Jeffrey Haar."

Gone is Mr. Haar's I'll-have-your-hide look. He now looks tan, well tailored, and in control.

"Thank you, Bob. It is my privilege to announce this morning that International Widget has joined with Phoenix Widget in a merger agreed upon last week and finalized yesterday afternoon. Phoenix Widget, as you may know, is the largest manufacturer of thermal widgets, with a 1984 gross sales volume of 77.3 million units. Terms of the final agreement, as filed this morning with the Securities & Exchange Commission, are detailed in a report that Mr. Heifetz made available to you a few moments ago.

"There will be no changes in management or personnel. All Phoenix Widget contracts will be handled according to their terms. I'll answer any questions you may have."

It's over in less than forty-five minutes. You watch the boss field the questions you've anticipated for him. The press leaves, and your life resumes. The boss and you are pleased.

A press conference is the release of a news story to a gathering of journalists who have been assembled for the sole purpose of receiving your information. It can be an informal conversation with representatives of two trade publications or a statement to an auditorium full of reporters and television crews. Its purpose is always to disperse information to all interested journalists at once.

The following is a checklist for press conferences.

1. Press conferences are inherently last-minute operations, but you will never be forgiven if you leave anything out. The first item on the checklist, then, is make a checklist.

2. Don't confuse a press conference with a press party. One is the release of news; the other is a junket that gets little serious coverage.

3. Don't leak any information. You must remain as neutral as Switzerland until the moment of the announcement. Otherwise, you might find coverage diminished when a news source breaks the story ahead of the announcement.

4. You must develop a carefully selected list of invitees. If the conference releases hard news, as most of them do, you don't want gossip columnists and feature writers from the Sunday supplement taking up space that should be allocated to other reporters.

5. While there are a number of ways to invite the press, the best method is probably by a series of hand-delivered announcements followed up by telephone calls to the list of invitees to be certain that they know about the conference and to query as to whether they will attend.

6. Morning conferences are best for most situations. Calling a conference for 10:00 or 11:00 A.M. allows the reporters enough time to file their stories.

7. Either have the event catered or provide your own coffee, pastries, mineral water, juice, and soft drinks. Wine and liquor are usually inappropriate for morning conferences.

8. Choose the right room. If it's too large, someone will say, "At a press conference that drew scant attention . . ." If it's too small, you'll read: ". . . The announcement was made in a cramped conference room at company headquarters." The room should be the right size for your estimated head count of attendees. Perhaps the most efficient method of balancing attendance with room size is to hold the conference in a hotel and discuss your expected attendance with the special events manager.

9. Make sure there are enough telephones available either in the conference room or nearby. Any hotel or convention

center can set you up with as many telephones as you feel are warranted.

10. If there is a videotaped demonstration, be sure to have copies available for each attending television station. Use ¾" tape.

11. Be sure to have plenty of heavy-duty extension cords and electrical outlets handy for the television crews. Camera operators prefer large and sturdy tables at the rear of the room so that they can shoot over the heads of reporters. If you have any doubts about the number of outlets needed, call in an electrician.

12. Sometimes the boss likes to ad lib beyond his prepared statement. Be certain that the quips don't get out of control. The best format is a short formal statement followed by a question-and-answer session.

13. Anticipate every possible question and go over each one of them carefully with the boss before the conference.

14. If possible, your company logo should fit on the front of the lectern over the hotel's name. Why should they get both the rent and the publicity? The lectern should be slightly elevated.

15. UPI and AP keep a "Day Book" of upcoming events, which they transmit early each morning to all subscribing broadcast stations, newspapers, and magazines. You should notify the Day Book editor in writing when you notify the wire-service reporters of the conference. This small step ensures that virtually every publicity source in your area will know about your conference.

16. The press usually arrives close to the appointed hour. Don't panic if they're a few minutes late.

17. Remember that a press conference is always in danger of failing. If a breaking news story such as a fire or bank

robbery occurs, or the mayor has his own last-minute press conference, you may find yourself eating the pastries and wishing you'd become a dentist. Keep the list of likely attendees and their direct telephone numbers handy in case you have to call people. Keep your employers informed of your progress. If it looks as if your story is about to be superseded, tell the boss immediately. Don't stand around nervously hoping for the best.

18. Have someone posted at the door to greet the reporters and hand them a detailed release.

Some love the action of a press conference, and some hate it. Wherever you stand, you'll certainly remember the morning for a very long time.

22
Trade
Publicity

It's Friday at Phoenix Widget, and the executives are getting restless. They've had lunch and they have been paid, but they cannot leave for the weekend without their early copies of *Widget Weekly*, the trade publication that defines their industry.

Theoretically, *WW*, as it's called in the widge biz, comes out on Monday with next Monday's date imprinted on the cover. But no self-respecting executive in the field can afford to wait for the inside story on what's happening. Right now, the mail room is late with the early copies.

Finally the van arrives at the door of the loading dock, and its driver is accosted by otherwise prim MBA's who serve as the company's junior executives. Their job of the moment is one of the most important tasks they perform all week, snaring *WW* for their bosses.

This ritual is repeated hundreds of times every week. The intensity of the wait varies with the pulse of the industry and the competence of its trade publication. Some fields not only wait until Monday but even then remain passive. Others require immediate harnessing of the information flow and gossip in order for executives to function properly. There are "name" colum-

₵imes BOOKS

TOUR SCHEDULE - DAVID K. SHIPLER - RUSSIA: Broken Idols, Solemn Dreams

Friday, November 18 -- CHICAGO TO DETROIT

Chicago Hotel: Detroit Hotel:
DRAKE   PONTCHARTRAIN
140 E. Walton Pl.   2 Washington Blvd.
Chicago, IL 60611   Detroit, MI 48226
(312) 787-2200   (313) 965-0200

Escort: Barbara Buckman
         (312) 649-6761

9:00 a.m.   Pick-up at hotel

9:45 a.m.   Radio interview, WIND, STEVE KING SHOW
(live from   625 N. Michigan, 3rd Floor
10 - 11 with   Contact: Sheryl Morton
call-ins)   (312) 751-5560

11:50 a.m.   TV interview, Cable News Network, TAKE TWO; national
(live from   Merchandise Mart Plaza, Rm 409
12-12:30)   Contact: Gail Evans
                                (404) 827-1500
                      Rick Smith will be on with you from their Washington studio.

12:45 p.m.   Lunch with Mike McGuire (foreign editor), Charles Madigan,
(until 2)   and Jim Gallagher of THE CHICAGO TRIBUNE; meet at the paper.
                      Contact: Mike McGuire
                                (312) 222-3232

2:15 p.m.   Radio interview, WCFL Radio, BOB & BETTY SANDERS
(until 2:45)   300 N. State St.
Taping   Contact: Denise Anderson
                                (312) 836-1000

3:00 p.m.   TV interview, PBS, KUP'S SHOW; national
(until 3:45)   233 N. Michigan
                      Contact: Todd Whitman
                                (312) 565-0957

5:35 p.m.   Depart Chicago, AMERICAN #214

7:30 p.m.   Arrive Detroit

11:00 p.m.   TV interview, PBS, LATENIGHT AMERICA; national
(live from   WTVS-TV, 7441 Second Blvd.
11:30 - 12)   Contact: Jan Zap
                                (313) 873-7200

The Tour Schedule. This sample of an actual tour schedule shows the possibilities of what can really be mined from a city in one day.

nists who are unknown to the public, but in plastics, tool and die, broadcasting, or publishing, the sun rises and sets with them. For some areas, a weekly publication is not enough. There are daily newspapers that are read ahead of any other publication.

Yet, trade publicity is often overlooked in planning campaigns. Clients who are willing to drop everything to do a backwater public-affairs radio show, snarl when their PR reps sell them to influential industry magazines.

As in any publicity endeavor, your first task is to define your market. Which industries do you really want to meet and who in them has to know about your product or idea? Since the titles of the publications are so endemic to their purpose (*Super Service Station*), and so numerous, you would be doing yourself a disservice to track down copies of all but the most influential among them.

Trade publications are often grateful for 8" × 10" or 5" × 7" photographs if they relate directly to the industry served. In some cases, such as recreation, the subject matter need only relate to the people involved.

House organs are often overlooked as a publicity source. A house organ is a company publication, usually edited by one or two people who hire free-lancers for paste-up, copy editing, and editorial chores. The exceptions are multinationals or other large corporations whose "in-house" publications are often larger than your local newspaper.

You're probably going to find seasoned magazine professionals at the helm when you query house organs or trade publications, so maintain the same level of professionalism that you would apply if you were approaching *Time*. The person you're trying to sell probably worked there and left because no mainstream slick could match the money and job security of a conglomerate. More to the point, this editor may still have friends at *Time*.

Trade publications are easily located in the reference room of your public library. It could be one of the most profitable trips you'll ever make. These people mean business.

23
Satellites and the New Technology

Your company finds that a competitor is going to release a version of the revolutionary new widget that has been in development at Phoenix Widget for the past eighteen months. They've called a press conference for tomorrow morning at 11:00. The boss is frantic. The Mini-Widge was his idea and he feels it was ripped off.

You suggest calling a press conference ahead of the competition, but even you feel that the haste and image of catch-up ball would be inappropriate. The boss is now kicking furniture. The time is 9:20 A.M., and you're not worried. You know something about satellites.

You ask the boss how he'd like to see a feature on the Mini-Widge on tonight's news. He says he'll do anything for you if you can pull such a thing off, but everyone knows that getting a videotape to television stations would not be possible. He's so sure of it that he promises you a Jaguar if the world knows about the Mini-Widge by tonight. You tell him they will but you'll need the cooperation of everyone in the top executive ranks of Phoenix. There can be no hide covering and protection of turf today. You get the go-ahead.

At 9:45 you've gone behind closed doors to call a satellite

178

news service. You want to know which transponders, invisible beacons, are available this afternoon. They'll call you back. Do that, you say, but get a crew to Phoenix Widget right away. You also tell them that you want a teleconference set up for company representatives in New York, Chicago, Dayton, Detroit, Cincinnati, and Los Angeles as soon as possible. You also tell him to prepare for a radio transmission. The satellite person whistles and bemoans the tallness of the order. He'll get right back to you.

The satellite producer is used to it. Every day clients call with some immediate disaster that has to be remedied by yesterday. They live in a world of tomorrow-may-never-come. They prefer twenty-four to thirty-six hours' notice, but this kind of request is not unprecedented.

Through the crack between the bottom of your office door and the carpet you see shadows of nervous footsteps. You know the boss and his entourage are in the outer office. You're thumbing through a Jaguar brochure. The phone intercom rings. The satellite people can deliver everything but Dayton on the teleconference. The crew is on the way.

The satellite people are busy notifying 380 commercial television stations and 1,500 cable systems that there will be an important feed representing a technological breakthrough this afternoon at 4:00. They spell out the satellite, transponder, and transponder number. They then use another system to notify 2,800 radio stations, most of them AM, that there is a news feature coming down on a revolutionary new widget. There are a number of sophisticated, computerized systems for reaching these outlets, and they all are in operation on a daily basis. Additionally, there's Telex, a private wire service, and commercial wire services that rent licenses of notification to individual satellite companies.

You call a meeting with the company's major executives at 10:45 A.M. Company representatives in New York, Chicago, Detroit, Cincinnati, and Los Angeles should proceed to the air-

port branch of the Sleepy Time Inn in each of these cities for a
one-way teleconference at 4:00 P.M. The Sleepy Time chain
has its own satellite contracts and jamming devices to ensure
that competitors don't monitor the closed-circuit television signals that today's technology makes possible. If you had a little
more time, you might have been able to pull off a two-way
conference where each branch officer would be free to ask
questions on camera but, on this kind of notice, a simple announcement of the day's events coupled with a transmission of
the new widget to the local executives will have to do. As it
stands, the telephone company's own Speakerphone technology will enable two-way conversation anyway.

The crew arrives and tapes the Mini-Widge, which has been
lighted and displayed against a satin backdrop in the company's showroom. A reporter takes notes and interviews the
president. Then he does a stand-up report with the Mini-
Widge in the background. He is a reporter but no journalist.
He is paid handsomely to narrate "infommercials," or broadcast stories offered free to stations with the dual purpose of providing information and plugging a product.

Since 1975, when Time, Inc., started using satellites to beam
Home Box Office directly to cable systems, public-relations
people have been able to form their own ad hoc networks.
They broadcast feature material directly to stations and conduct follow-up surveys to report usage to clients. Reporters
often trade in their underpaid jobs in journalism for the more
lucrative call of electronic publicity. Major radio networks
such as Associated Press, United Press International, Mutual,
and National Public Radio rent satellite time for closed-circuit
distribution of feature material to their affiliates.

The satellite people rush to the nearest studio with "uplink-
ing" facilities, meaning that their finished reports can be transmitted to a communications satellite in orbit 23,500 miles
above the equator. The signal is then returned to earth and
picked up by the stations' "downlinking" receiving dishes. Sat-

ellite technology is inexpensive, clear, and efficient. Prior to their recent elevation to widespread usage, signals were transmitted by high-fidelity telephone lines that were efficient but beyond anyone's budget for the type of project undertaken in the hypothetical case of Phoenix Widget. Let's continue with the day.

At 3:00, the television stations receive the transmission of a ninety-second report that introduces the new widget. They also receive a full half-hour of repeated stock shots of the Mini-Widge with computer graphics underscoring the name and model number. Of 380 stations, only 22 at first thought the idea was "revolutionary" enough for use on the preciously budgeted evening news time. Then Cable News Network decided to go with the story. That inspired NBC to scan its tapes for your transmission (networks monitor these feeds but don't usually pick them up) for use as a "kicker" story, a human-interest feature placed at the end of a newscast. UPI and AP took notice, and by morning the boss was in New York shuttling between the *Today* show and *Good Morning America* for interviews. Each insisted on being first and exclusive, but you managed to work a deal where you would do them both within an hour, although you had to exclude *CBS Morning News*. No problem, it turns out, because they never called anyway.

Meanwhile, the radio feature, broadcast to news directors of National Public Radio, Associated Press, and Mutual Broadcasting System stations, produced an estimated response of more than 700 radio stations, or 25 percent of those receiving the feed. It was an extraordinarily successful endeavor, and it seems as though everyone you know heard something about the Mini-Widge en route home from work.

At 4:00 the Dayton rep managed to make it to the airport in Cincinnati for a teleconference. It was an uncomplicated and informal presentation where the boss talked about the Mini-Widge and a separate camera displayed it. A teleconference is

merely a less pizazzy version of Ted Koppel's *Nightline*, where
people talk to each other from remote television locations. The
reps had called key distributors by 5:00. The Widget gossip
channels move quickly, and by 6:00 the competition knew it
was beaten. They proceeded with their 11:00 A.M. press conference the next day, but the resulting publicity was purely in
the also-ran category. You decide that cranberry would be a
nice color for your Jaguar sedan.

The scenario is only a little farfetched and by no means impossible. The apparatus described, including satellite link-ups
with major radio networks and skyward beaming of hotel
chains, is in place and ready for you. Usually, it takes an extra
day to happen, and it is unlikely that NBC will take footage directly from a public-relations satellite beacon. More likely,
networks will dispatch their own crews once inspired by the
feed.

Today and *Good Morning America* rarely use the same
guest, but they have been known to do so with such high-
volume news generators as movies and celebrity interviews.
If a Mini-Widge had a profound impact on technology or a
strong news value, the example would be an understatement.
Teleconferences of the magnitude described take a few days to
set up, but all hotel chains using satellites agree that the
Phoenix Widget scenario is a plan that will soon be available as
described.

Electronic publicity is the generation of exposure through
the use of today's technology. You can make a videotape and
beam it anywhere in the world. You can make an audio tape
and ensure its delivery to thousands of radio stations. You can
star in your own cable talk show and set up a network where it
travels from one cable system to another for months. The following is a brief introduction and guide to using electronics to
assist in your campaign.

RADIO

Whether your publicity is electronic or conventional, radio remains your best buddy. You can get on the radio either by soliciting individual stations through a postcard mailing or by satellite. Mutual, National Public Radio, UPI, and AP sell satellite time on their networks as do independent contractors such as New York's Audio Features Inc. In any satellite transaction, the regularity of the feed is as important as the potential usage of the information you send. Thus, you need to be part of a beacon that reaches stations every day.

TELEVISION

A ninety-second feature is probably the best unit of transmission for television. If you can find a video facility that will produce a good stand-up news feature, stations will carry it. Unlike radio, where major-market pickup is a stronger possibility, television distribution favors smaller communities. But if you can make a good tape, you can get it on the air.

CABLE

Cable productions are usually implemented in twenty-eight-minute units without commercial interruption. Use public service announcements available free from any large nonprofit organization to break the program into short units. Whether you use satellites or conventional distribution such as postcard mailing and telephone calls, cable will put you on the air. The trick is to interest the cable networks (of which there are dozens). Most cable systems are rigged for satellite reception.

CHOOSING A SATELLITE CORPORATION

All commercial satellite companies can put your radio or video image into space, but the difference between the pros and the hustlers is the frequency of contact with broadcast and cable operations. If you're thinking of moving into any area of satellite distribution, ask to see a report of actual pickup for recent projects. Anyone unwilling or unable to provide such information should not be considered. A common hustle in the satellite world is, "We reach more than two thousand cable systems." Never mind what they reach. When you start from 23,500 miles above the equator, your signal *reaches* everyone. But it's no more effective than a photograph without that report and without frequent communication and goodwill between the satellite company and the participating stations.

TELECONFERENCING

Teleconferencing is the live transmission of nonbroadcast television signals by satellite. A business teleconference can involve two branch managers of a company discussing sales strategies from New York and Los Angeles, or it can consist of a network of fifty participants from all over the world.

The field is wide open, and your best opening shot with it is to check the Yellow Pages and request a meeting. Names you know and have worked with for a long time, such as Holiday Inn and AT&T, are very active in the field. Teleconferencing is becoming sophisticated in its production techniques with graphics, sets, talent, and technology that parallel those of broadcast networks. It's also a good way to get a bunch of reps together without flying them anywhere. It will probably never replace the annual convention, but teleconferencing is a workable alternative to business trips that no one wants to take.

MAKING THE TAPE

"What kind of videotape do you want, ma'am?"
"What do you mean, what kind of videotape do I want?"
"By that, I mean what format?"
"What's a format?"

"Half-inch, three-quarter-inch, one-inch, or two-inch?"

"Half-inch, I think."

"You can't think. You have to know, ma'am."

"Hey, Fred. Is it half-inch? Yeah, half-inch."

"Half-inch Beta or half-inch VHS?"

"Beta."

"Beta one, Beta two, or Beta three?"

That is a realistic approximation of what will happen when you have a tape made that will fit the home video machine attached to your television set. Imagine the fun in trying to assess a video studio that makes broadcast-quality tape. The first item on your agenda is to visit a video company and listen to an orientation. You might also consider taking a course. If you're going to work in video at all, and you probably are, you'll get fleeced if you fall into the jargon of video technology.

Don't assume that the nice person who shows you around the production facility has any idea of what he's doing. He might be able to spout acronyms and shorthand, but producing a good video is still a matter of instinct and judgment. That, you have as much as anyone.

If you decide to do any television, you'll be asked what kind of visuals you are able to provide. If you are in a position to come in with a ¾" videotape, so much the better. But price it out before you give anyone the go-ahead, get the cost in writing, ask for references, check those references, and hold the company to its price. You should never spend more than a few hundred dollars for a ninety-second to two-minute tape shot in a studio. If a crew has to leave the premises and come to your house, start the estimate at $1,000 to $1,500. Never surrender control to someone who convinces you that you're the layperson and he or she is the expert. You've been watching television all your life. That is all the expertise you need to supervise your own production.

24
Publicity Potpourri

Several publicity endeavors that probably fit more comfortably into the category of promotion are worthy of our attention.

SPEECHES

A speech differs from a press conference in that the speaker is addressing a general audience rather than a group of journalists for the release of a specific story.

Conventional wisdom in publicity texts has been that we should speak whenever we can to spread the word on an idea. But speeches can be dangerous. Most people are much better one-to-one than one-to-many, and if you're one of them, either don't speak at all or begin in very small rooms.

Most speakers try to break the ice with a funny story. That too can be a loaded revolver, because if it falls flat, your confidence will drop and the audience will drop you. The slightest betrayal of tentativeness will result in an awful moment when you're barely under way but can see people shifting in their seats or looking at their watches.

On the other side, however, you should know that a successful speech will make you feel like a Beatle in 1964. The crowd will lean forward, and you'll see people nod as you confidently rattle off your points. The question-and-answer period that follows the speech will further your momentum as will the inevitable gaggle of well-wishers who will come to the podium when you're done.

There are books and speech coaches for you to consult. Virtually all expert sources will advise plenty of rehearsal, even if you're one of those anointed souls with an ability to speak extemporaneously. In fact, most extemp artists got that way by hammering in their techniques through rehearsal. If you saw a professional lecturer in Phoenix on Monday and followed this speaker to Chicago on Tuesday, you would almost certainly see the same speech complete with funny story, pauses, and inflections. The answers to the audience questions will even be the same.

Be certain that a release reaches the appropriate media sources well in advance to assure a good turnout and, if you can swing it, try for a follow-up story.

POSTERS AND PAMPHLETS

Benjamin Franklin and Thomas Paine used pamphlets successfully enough to influence history. You are not likely to get that far, but one never knows. As always, there are a couple of dangers.

The first is expense. As soon as your sense of aesthetics tells you that your pamphlet or poster just has to be in color, you're going for broke and you're probably going to get there. Multicolored printed pamphlets require a delicate and time-consuming blend of tones and inks. The final result looks great, but the handsomeness is reflected in the cost. Printers tend to be very accurate in their assessment of costs, and you should consult with several before going ahead. Persuade an artistic friend to illustrate the master artwork that printers refer to as mechanicals. A mechanical is a completed design layout that is ready for reproduction by a printer.

Another pitfall is a potential brush with the law. Handouts litter, and the policeman won't necessarily be your friend if you distribute them in a public place. What usually happens is that someone takes your pamphlet and throws it away ten seconds later. Instead, try to enlist the aid of established businesses to display a small handful of your pamphlets at a time. If the pile is too large, someone will take the whole collection. No one knows why, but it always happens. Maybe there are children in Europe starving for propaganda.

Posters are clearly illegal in most public places. The law is also with the property owner if you paste something on the side of her or his building. There are public bulletin boards in supermarkets and laundromats, but they often aren't big enough for serious display of posters. Make sure you really have somewhere to place your posters before you give the printer a green light.

WRITING

Your newspaper will always welcome a query if you have a flair for writing and wish to offer an article. Remember to query before writing and to begin with a clear idea of the word count. If they call for 500 words, don't give them 1,500 and assume they'll edit to suit their available space. They are as short of time as they are of space. They might just junk the piece. You can take your cause beyond the local newspaper to magazines, Sunday supplements, newsletters, and other publications. Even if you are not inclined to write, perhaps someone can organize your ideas on paper for you.

Besides the placement of articles, the value of a publication's letters column cannot be overstated. Most newspapers and magazines welcome readers' letters.

You may chuckle at advice columns, but you don't see any

shortage of them. Whether you're approaching Mary Ellen with hints, Dear Abby for advice, or Sylvia Porter with a money matter, you'll find an instant national audience for your pitch if you are fortunate enough to have your letter printed.

EDITORIAL REPLIES

"This station welcomes opposing views from responsible spokespersons."

You've heard that a thousand times at the end of a radio or television editorial, and you've probably groaned as someone from the community got on the air in response to an editorial you never heard, or cared about, in the first place. But you'll notice that the responsible spokesperson is responding in a time slot that may be worth ten grand per minute. The FCC, even in these deregulated times, scrutinizes a station's response to issues in the community, and if all editorial replies are sandwiched between the "Thought for Today" and the national anthem, someone is going to get called on it.

If you have a genuine concern, write to the station and request an airing. Don't be surprised if you get it.

PARTIES

"I spent three grand entertaining those freeloaders and didn't even get a mention! Never again!"

Some don't get off that cheaply. Probably the most classic mistake people make is expecting direct coverage from a party. If you're in a smaller community, you'll get your party on the appropriate page or perhaps even on television, but in cities there's just too much major news to allow for coverage of all social events. Parties can serve other, still valid, functions, however.

Attention is what you get for your money. The press will attend and know what you're selling even if they can't write up the party itself. It is a common experience for a reporter to say,

Mr and Mrs William Colford,
Chairman of the Board at Phoenix Widget, Inc.,
invite you to a dinner and demonstration to view
the revolutionary new
MINI-WIDGE

Wednesday, March 14
6:30 p.m.
Cafe du Soir
One Des Plaines Avenue
Racine, Wisconsin

R.S.V.P.
Nancy Howe
414 352-6000

You are cordially invited
to a cocktail reception
to celebrate the publication of
HOW TO GET PUBLICITY
by William Parkhurst
Times Books

Tuesday, July 30th ~ 5:30 p.m.
The Four Seasons
51 East 52nd Street

R.S.V.P.
Cindy Adelman
212 224-4949

The Party Invitation.
Many invitations
adopt the kind of
simple elegance shown
above. Of course, the
possibilities for design
are limitless, depend-
ing on whom or what
you're promoting.

"Bob, I'd like to talk to you more about this. Can you call me in the morning?" Or, weeks later you'll receive a call when a reporter is at work on a feature that applies. The grand opening of an automobile dealership might not be considered news, but the owner might be interviewed later on the topic of the increasing value of used cars.

Parties don't have to be expensive. If you can coax either a business friend or a nonprofit organization to donate the real estate (a restaurant banquet room, a church activity center, etc.), you've immediately shaved hundreds off the budget. Friends who have specialty dishes can help with the hors d'oeuvres. But don't do anything that looks like a scrimp job. Don't run into a card shop and pick up an invitation that reads, "We're having a party at _____." Press people like name places, whether the name happens to be a fancy residence or a restaurant. If you are faced with a choice between renting a banquet room at a big-name restaurant at a discount or sending the press to Uncle Morris's Bar and Grill, go with the status or go without.

Printers will show you a variety of invitation options, and you can probably find a good one to meet your budget. Perhaps a friend who does calligraphy will make the master invitation.

All the rules in Chapter 20 apply to parties. Make sure you don't schedule on the date of a conflicting event, and make certain that your list is carefully planned to reach the press people you need. Journalists work hour by hour and might have a difficult time responding too far ahead of time.

With imagination and careful planning, you may find a party to be a valuable addition to your campaign.

25
The Nationals

"A no is as good as a yes," one publicist says to the other after the second drink of an expense-account lunch.

"Better still if it's a quick no," replies the colleague, and they both smile.

Their clients would want to boil these two hotshots in oil if they overheard this conversation about booking network television shows. The clients, however, would not be interpreting the shoptalk correctly. It's not that they don't work hard and fiercely on behalf of the companies they represent; they are merely conversing in a shorthand that bespeaks the travails of their fastest lane.

If the average major-market talk-show office gets plowed under with material and telephone calls every day, the network programs get avalanched beyond the comprehension of those who have not seen the daily parade of messengers, overnight express delivery people, mail by the sack, telegrams (even singing ones), and every conceivable gimmick to grab attention.

Nuts show up at NBC in Burbank demanding to see Carson, as though he hangs out in the lobby just waiting to greet mothers with little girls who can sing "Tomorrow." Black hosts are invited to scholarship fund raisers in the ghetto so often that they would be unemployed if they accepted one thirty-second of them. After struggling against great odds to make it, they're not thrilled having to tell someone calling from a tiny Baptist church on the outskirts of Atlanta to "talk to my agent." But what choice do they really have? Jewish celebrities are asked to give up their $10,000-per-performance fees to show up at Bar Mitzvahs and Hadassah groups, while Catholics get pulled toward this or that diocese.

The parade of demands works against the program's own ghoulish time and energy requirements as too few staffers work to put out a show. Count the number of guests on *Today, Good Morning America,* or *CBS Morning News* and you'll find fifteen or more interviews each *day.* Most of these are filled with newsmakers or "name" interviews, not because the shows are in love with them but because we are. If we all demanded to see more unknown talking heads, they would be there. Thus, one should not be phenomenally surprised that people get the process backward. They think they can go on network shows and become famous. The reality is that you need to become well known in a particular area, pay some dues with other forms of publicity, and step up to national recognition. Then you'll be *more* famous. More famous is the key.

That is not to say that the network shows don't want you. A network, after all, is but a string of stations. The first contact, then, is your local program director or station manager of a network affiliate. Meet him at the club, play tennis, coach Little League, or whatever, but get to know people at your local television station. They are your New York contact. Networks pay phenomenal homage to their affiliates, and if the station manager of a local outlet writes to the network on your behalf, you are almost guaranteed a fair hearing. You are not guaranteed a booking, but someone will look at your videotape and perhaps arrange a pre-interview. That's more clout than you could ever buy.

Sometimes you don't even need a station executive; if you make friends with the contact at a talk show where you've done well and have been asked back several times, that person will write on your behalf. But the one question you must answer first is, "How unusual is my story?" Be objective about it. National programs want something fresh, an idea that they don't see every day, or a trend that is in such vogue that any new twist is welcome.

"Timely" is the word you'll hear most often when national media decision makers discuss the unending search for new ideas. Pet rocks were timely in 1975. Hula hoops were timely in 1958. During the Christmas season of 1983, Cabbage Patch dolls were big news. There are no easy rules to assess the timeliness of your idea, but you'll find that network people will have a strong sense of its value to their audiences. In the early seventies, for example, anyone who could talk to plants and claim they talked back had a good chance of being booked. Rule number one in booking the nationals is to *know what they're doing*.

Next, you must find out who will be receiving your materials. The reference will offer names, but, in the case of nationals, you're better off calling the show. Don't ask for anyone specific on the first pass:

"NBC, good morning."

"The *Today* show, please."

"Anyone in particular?"

"Just the general office for now, thank you."

"I'll connect you."

"*Today.*"

"Good morning. I have a pet ape who can play 'Chopsticks' underwater while wearing scuba gear. We perform at shopping centers throughout Michigan to call attention to the inhumane treatment of chimpanzees in our nation's zoos. I'd like to send clippings and a videotape for a possible booking during

National Animal Week, March twenty-first through twenty-sixth. To whose attention should that be addressed?"
"Very interesting. Send it to the attention of Mr. _____."

Or,

"Send it to my attention, and I'll see that the appropriate producer gets it."
Bingo. You have a name. Usually, the call won't even run that long, but the conversation demonstrates that a "Chopsticks"-playing ape is unusual, and it's more appealing if he's playing his tune for a purpose. The ape is more attractive still if there is a nationally designated week where a lot of people arc working for a common purpose.
"*Today* is a news and feature program," says its book editor, Emily Boxer. "We are always focused on the timeliness of a topic in evaluating its potential."
The next lesson is derived from a hackneyed notion that "creative" press agentry is going to help. Don't send a Strip-O-Gram, a balloon bouquet, or a teddy bear that reads "Hug me and book Bob Madden." Send good materials, make follow-up calls, and persist. You would be wasting a videotape if you sent it without an invitation to do so. While the shows value a recording that reveals your talents under the lights of a previous interview, the tape should be offered in a cover letter or telephone conversation. If you are fortunate enough to get a quick "No," go on to the next show. Foot-in-the-door, high-pressure salesmanship is apt to work against you.
The most exasperating moments come when a show staffer says, "Yeah. I think we're interested. Call back Tuesday." You start telling relatives about the positive response, and you wonder how many of the high school classmates who called you a nerd will catch your act on television. By Tuesday you can barely speak.
"Call Thursday," the person now says. On Thursday, you get booked, and high beyond the range of any chemical con-

cocted by either civilization or nature. On Friday, you get un-
booked and never again get through to the person who said
"yes."

A national booking can become unglued right up to the hour
of your scheduled appearance. You may get all the way to the
Tonight Show green room (it's not really green—it's come to be
a general term to describe the anteroom of a show) only to be
bumped and never rescheduled. Then you have to call everyone you know with a lame explanation of why you failed to be
included. It's the ultimate case of don't-count-your-chickens.

Other frustrations include the switching from a live to a
taped segment at the last minute. Then, one of two things happens: the tape never runs, or you receive a call from a cousin
three thousand miles away who tells you that you were on television that morning, the first day you decided not to watch.

As plentiful as they are, these are the exceptions. Usually the
show says yes, you show up, and you go on. But you should
know that when you're dealing with the bigs, you're in show
business. Anyone who has made it in that very tough world of
entertainment has been through your little trauma a hundred
times in a hundred different ways. If one compiled a list of
names bumped from national shows, it would read like the
Celebrity Register. Bear that in mind if you do share the green-
room couch with a movie star and he or she is a trifle aloof. National publicity is a very serious business to a public figure.

You can do your own booking on network shows, but it's better to have someone else endure the process on your behalf.
The exception is *Sixty Minutes,* which is not so much a booking
as a miracle.

THE PRE-INTERVIEW

Unless you're a celebrity or newsmaker, go for the pre-interview instead of the booking. You'll be taken a lot more
seriously if you request a fair hearing of your pitch. The

pre-interview is a long way from the actual scheduling of a segment, but it makes contact between the show and you, and gives the producer or talent coordinator something to remember. Usually, they'll agree to a telephone conversation, especially if you live a long way from the studio.

Be especially mindful of visuals during the conversation. If you have a wonderful tape, slides, or other such material, remind the person interviewing you of them. Don't assume that mentioning them in a pitch letter will be enough. Once the interview is concluded, ask for an answer one way or another *as soon as the person has one. Not this minute.* Too many people conclude their interview and say, "Well, how did I do and when do I get booked?" Bookings are usually decided in meetings.

YOUR TAPE

The national programs may not need it, but you should always have a ¾" tape of yourself being interviewed, either in an edited montage of several good performances or in an intact local segment. Most network shows prefer an unedited conversation. They'll allow for the fact that your cowlick stood up that day, your pancake was smudged, or that your interviewer was a dolt. They need only an idea of your strength as a conversationalist. *Don't send the whole show,* complete with local commercials and other guests. If you request a copy of the interview from the local station, it might not be edited. Take it to a video house equipped to deal with ¾" tape and spend a few dollars to clip out the extraneous program material. Even though most programs are equipped to deal with Beta or VHS, it's still a more professional approach to use ¾" as a format. Remember, you're trying out for the Yankees here.

If you have succeeded in local publicity, moved to regional and major market outlets, and are now ready to take a shot at the big time, the following guidelines may help. Because shows come and go rapidly, we have confined the selection to a few long-standing giants that are likely to remain on the air or in publication for some time. Media staffers and publicists with lengthy national track records were consulted. They don't always agree on what works, but they agree that success with the nationals hinges on a firm grasp of realities in the business. Logic points out that the major shows and publications usually won't be able to accommodate your solicitation but that they need a constant infusion of fresh ideas to survive. Suggestions are *never unwelcome*, not anywhere. Write before you call. Send good materials and offer visuals. Live with no for an answer and try again with another topic. Beyond that, no one knows how to book nationals.

Today
NBC
30 Rockefeller Plaza
New York, NY 10020

The *Today* show invented morning network television, and most of us can recall before-school images of Garroway, Garagiola, Walters, astronauts, authors, and enough faces to fill Yankee Stadium if they could be brought together for a reunion.

"I suggest that people be very specific in approaching us," says Emily Boxer. "In my department, we handle books, and if someone is offering a book on child care, for example, we need to know immediately why this author's ideas stand out against the ten thousand other books on the topic."

Today people will look at ¾" inch videotapes if they become interested in your idea. Don't send them cold. The program's various departments pre-interview prospective guests and keep a sharp eye open for interesting visuals. Don't worry about an idea having been done by the program before; it certainly will have been covered at some point. Do keep in mind that *Today* is a news program and always has been. What has your idea to do with the headlines and cultural trends? If nothing, they probably won't make the booking.

Remember that *Today*, like all live shows, relies heavily on your ability to speak. According to producer Marty Ryan, the ability to articulate an idea is the most important prerequisite for getting on the air. "We pre-interview all of our feature guests," he says. "We find that many people have interesting subjects to discuss on paper but cannot 'talk' the same points on live television."

Good Morning America
ABC
7 West 66th St.
New York, NY 10023

"All the morning shows on network television move at least close to the speed of sound in their booking," says a publicist who frequently books *Today*, *Good Morning America*, and *CBS Morning News*. "But on most mornings, *GMA* books at the speed of light."

Since it first appeared on ABC in 1975, *Good Morning America* has maintained a pace that can be life-threatening to its production staff. You can get a call on Tuesday night and find yourself on the air by seven the next morning, either in the studio or by satellite from your hometown. You can be booked three weeks ahead of time and find yourself bumped at the last minute. It all evens out. While all three network shows follow the headlines in the rearrangement of their guest lineups, *GMA* is especially well known for quicksilver changes. You will want to kick someone if you're bumped after choosing a new outfit, but you may also get booked suddenly after you've decided that national television will elude you forever.

In the early days, "folksy" was the watchword for the type of segment favored by *GMA*, the only program of the three morning shows that is not under the aegis of the network's news department. If you had a topic that would appeal to a more urban and white-collar audience, you stopped first at *Today*, while your banjo-plucking national finalists or your hamster race was thought to be *GMA* fodder. The faint traces of those images exist among some publicists today, although NBC's Willard Scott announces ham-and-bean suppers in Cedar Rapids with the resonance of a cattle auctioneer, and Charles Kuralt of CBS enjoys rock star-style adoration among "plain folks." *Good Morning America*, meanwhile, gets as newsy as either of its competitors.

Write and see if they write back.

CBS Morning News
524 West 57th St.
New York, NY 10019

There's really not a lot of difference in the actual booking of any of the three morning programs, but one should remember that CBS people are always conscious of their network's dominance in the history of television news. CBS was Murrow's network, and Cronkite's. *The Selling of the Pentagon* inflamed Nixon administration officials in one of the big controversies of the early seventies. This heritage forms an invisible guide in every corner of the news department. Just as *The New York Times* doesn't print comics, *Morning* people are tweedier, and less amused by anything that feels too induced by public relations.

Sixty Minutes
CBS
524 West 57th St.
New York, NY 10019

"We look for a news story, a real news story that can stand up to thorough substantiation by our staff," says Don Hewitt, the legendary executive producer of this Sunday evening American institution. Things happen when *Sixty Minutes* agrees to do your story. You might be in jail for a crime you did not commit and you'll get out. You might find crowds of people dying to buy what you're selling on Monday morning, or you might find yourself with no business at all, depending on how the piece goes. Either way, Americans do not take this program casually.

Don't send reams of material or copies of the documents that you believe will change the course of history. Write a letter. They read their mail at *Sixty Minutes*, much more carefully than you might expect.

"I tell people that they should write rather than call," Hewitt says. His staff must contend with a large volume of mail, but they're used to it. They're also accustomed to finding their stories in the mailbag, even though there's no way that most inquiries can be accommodated. Hewitt himself is a rapid fire mail reader.

As is the case with all national shows, you should pay close attention to the type of programming currently on the air— what Ed seems to be doing these days, what Morley is up to in the eighties, and what makes Harry twinkle. You have to look closely, because there is a danger of typecasting. Mike Wallace doesn't always favor assault, and Harry Reasoner is far from cheerful on many of his stories. Many who have been interviewed by Morley Safer would sooner nap on a hot stove.

Next, check out the producers. Each piece is put together by a particular producer—whose name appears at the beginning of the segment—who may be right for your story. A single-page letter to this person may be far more productive than a batch of urgent telegrams to Don Hewitt. (Don't, by the way, assume that telegrams or mailgrams are going to propel you to the top of the morning mail. They're as common as chewing-gum wrappers around these shows.)

If you interest the program, you will spend a lot of time with a crew prior to the arrival of a correspondent. They will follow you around, check your story thoroughly, and scrutinize every surface. You will know them by name. When the correspondent arrives, you will probably spend several hours under the lights being interviewed. There will be follow-up calls, more interviews (probably by the producers), and miles of footage for a thirteen-minute segment. Don't expect a lot of notice before your piece goes on the air. *Sixty Minutes* works very close to the wire.

It starts with an idea and a letter. If you think you really have something, go to it.

The David Susskind Show
1271 Ave. of the Americas
New York, NY 10020

This program has been on the air long enough to have featured Nikita Khrushchev. If the three morning network shows have seen it all, this one has probed it all with artesian-well depth. David Susskind favors panels of people with divergent views discussing a common issue or problem, preferably with some controversy. It is one of the few national shows that welcomes and actively seeks the noncelebrity.

First, write a letter. If you hear from the show, you will be pre-interviewed extensively, sometimes by several staff members. This is probably the most rigorous pre-interview in television, and you shouldn't be shocked or disappointed if it doesn't work out. In most cases, it doesn't. The questions will come fast with many interruptions, and you may find that you pass muster only to learn that other potential panelists didn't. The idea, then, might be shelved temporarily or permanently.

Everything has to fit together. If it works out, your program will stay on the air for many months. The *Susskind Show* is "bicycle" syndicated, meaning that the tapes are shipped from station to station, rather than distributed by a single satellite transmission. If the show was really good, meaning that every-one on your panel and the one that followed (usually each show features two) sparkled, the show may be repeated, and you'll be on television two years or more after the original taping.

Donahue
630 North McClurg Court
Chicago, IL 60611

"We've done that show, but thank you for thinking of us," is a common response from the highly professional staff of this long-running daytime giant. "That show" would refer to her-pes, open marriage, post-college sons and daughters moving back home, the Moral Majority, or media influence—any issue of our day. You have to come upon a trend early to sell it to the *Donahue* show before the staff pursues it without the benefit of a publicity pitch.

People often forget that the show is a partnership between Phil Donahue and the studio audience. Your idea must lend it-self to a multiheaded interview conducted principally by the audience, usually women, who sometimes wait for two years for their tickets. You're also going to be asked some very probing questions by Donahue himself, with the occasional telephone call from the viewing audience in New York, where the show is now seen live every day. Very often, you will have guests who differ from your viewpoint assaulting you from right and left. This program is not for the passive, but it is one of the most exciting experiences you can have. There is one topic per hour and one hour per day, so the odds of getting on aren't the best. On the other hand, you don't have to be a "name," and you can become one quickly after the exposure.

The *Donahue* staff takes exceptional care in perusing ideas. Most publicists see the program as an oasis of courtesy among the nationals. But senior producer Patricia McMillen, who has

been supervising the booking of guests since the sixties, warns
that professionalism has to be a two-way street:

"The biggest mistake people make in approaching us is being
too aggressive once we've decided not to pursue an idea. We
have a strong sense of what we feel is important for our audience," she says.

People who work with the show often respect the staff's sense
of what will work and take no graciously. Ms. McMillen reports that the program now uses more guests per program than
in previous years, when it was common for Phil to spend his
daily hour with his studio audience and a single guest.

The *Tonight Show*
NBC
2000 West Alameda Ave.
Burbank, CA 91523

Our lives could take a slight turn that will interest Donahue,
Susskind, or the network morning shows. That's comforting in
an "only in America" way. It is equally reassuring to know that
we can relax at night and look in on a show that is a members-
only club for people who have made it. Unknown talking
heads require a little bit of work on the viewer's part. Who is
this person again? What is she saying? You have to strain and
catch the credits on the lower third of the screen. But *Tonight*
is for celebrities, and we can doze off watching Johnny and Ed
do the same act they've done for more than two decades.

The *Tonight Show* is closed to most of us, especially since the
program switched from a ninety-minute format to an hour. If
you accept that no is the norm, there are several publicity options open to you.

You might write and propose a "desk segment" that will plug
your idea or product during the top of the show when Johnny
and Ed (or Joan and Ed, or Joan and Doc . . . whoever!)
warm up together before the guests come out.

"In Missoula, Montana *(applause from the audience, probably from a single Montanan in attendance that night)*, there's a company that makes . . . and I have it right here in this newspaper clipping, Ed . . . birth-control devices for roosters."

If you are an entertainer who feels ready—that means a few years of nightly professional entertainment rather than a couple of high points when you sang "Send in the Clowns" at a family wedding—you can cite credentials and ask the staff to look at a ¾" videotape. Steve Lawrence and Eydie Gorme, George Carlin, Joan Rivers, Steve Martin, and many others were once unknowns who needed a break and got it on this show. But they were ready for the audition, and that is the difference between the amateurs and professionals who try out for the program. Few are called, fewer are chosen, but there is always the chance.

If you send in copies of clippings that show you in an amusing light, you may be pre-interviewed. If you make news in an offbeat way, as in landing a hot-air balloon in Lake Michigan by mistake, or do something that Middle Americans would consider heroic, you might find yourself in the ultimate talk-show seat.

Tonight isn't there to drum up interest in cancer research, or to discuss seriously nuclear agreements with the Soviet Union, unless you happen to be Henry Kissinger. It is there so people can forget such weightiness and have a few laughs at the end of their day. Respect that if you're going after this particular brass ring.

According to the program's senior talent coordinator, Robert Dolce, "We're always on the prowl for what is fresh, original, and entertaining—something we haven't done before and something that will entertain Johnny and amuse our viewers."

Based on the program's advertising rates, figure $420,000 worth of exposure if you do capture Johnny's imagination.

The Larry King Show
Mutual Broadcasting System
1755 S. Jefferson Davis Highway
Arlington, VA 22202

The Larry King Show reaches out to America's night people, a huge segment of the population that no campaign can afford to overlook. Shift workers, police, medical personnel, and those of us who have never gotten around to going to bed at a "decent" hour listen often.

The program's booking office keeps regular hours. If you don't get scheduled as a guest, you can call in on a segment of the show called "Open Phone America," and Larry will probably give you a couple of national minutes to say your piece. Though you will need a lot of patience to get through, going on the radio as a caller is always worth the wait. Keep that in mind for local as well as national exposure.

The Wire Services:

United Press International
220 East 42nd St.
New York, NY 10018

The Associated Press
50 Rockefeller Plaza
New York, NY 10020

The two megasources of UPI and AP are all but invisible to the average news consumer. However, they supply your local newspaper, radio, or television station with news by teletype twenty-four hours daily.

The first step to take is to approach the wire service bureau in the city nearest you. Your state capital probably has an office, and you'll certainly find one in any major city. Handle the situation with the same finesse you would summon when approaching a network; make a general call to determine a name, write to that person, and make a follow-up call. Captioned photos are often welcome enough to be beamed around the world via satellite.

If you have a problem getting through to the regional office, try writing to, or calling, the home bases (addresses above). You have nothing to lose.

The New York Times
229 West 43rd St.
New York, NY 10036

The New York Times is grouped among the nationals because of its undisputed status as the newspaper of record. At times, it seems that the whole world is attempting to place a story in its newsrooms.

A letter to an individual is always more effective than an anonymous pitch, and, with *The Times*, you can get a solid feel for the responsibilities of various writers after a couple of weeks. You would limit your chances, however, if you wrote to a particular reporter rather than his or her editor. As always, call the newsroom, ask where to send your correspondence, and send it. You won't get chased away or cursed at if you make a polite follow-up call. However, you should take no for an answer and let them get back to work once the decision has been reached.

Never underestimate your opportunity to get into *The Times* by writing either a letter or a query to the editor of the "Op-Ed" page (so named because of the positioning opposite the editorial page).

People
1271 Ave. of the Americas
New York, NY 10020

People staffers are not necessarily far away in New York, Chicago, or Los Angeles. The magazine keeps a careful eye on trends, wherever they occur. You may be assured that there's a *People* correspondent, probably free-lance, scanning the publicity in your area.

Read the magazine carefully and take note of where you might fit, bearing in mind that *People* thrives on recognizable names. When you find the section that seems to fit your situation ("Couples," "Sequel," or whatever), send your clippings or a letter to the appropriate department and ask if there is a correspondent in your region whom you might be able to contact.

It's always a long shot but always well worth the effort when it pays off.

"The stringer network is very important to *People*," says longtime senior editor Landon Y. Jones, now managing editor of *Money* magazine, *People*'s sister publication. "In every major city we have people who do not work for the magazine but contribute to it. They send in clippings that are taken so seriously that I would say at least three or four stories per issue originate in this fashion."

USA Today
Box 500
Washington, DC 20044
(202) 872-8329 or (703) 276-3400

Since September of 1982, *USA Today* has quickly taken hold as "the nation's newspaper" and has managed to cover the whole country as if it were a ham-and-bean supper at the

Grange Hall. The publication is colorful and friendly. It some-how takes the edge off the horror of morning news.

Like *People*, *USA Today* relies heavily on contributions of local free-lancers. You're probably no more than a traffic light away from a correspondent.

When you read the paper, you'll see that there is a section called "Across the USA," which is a community bulletin board featuring news from your state. You'll also notice that your local high school football tournament is covered in the sports section alongside news from the major leagues.

For more prominently displayed coverage, including one of the paper's trademark color photos, the editors advise submitting to the appropriate department. We suggest a phone call to the assignment desk in Washington for the name of the proper person. There's no point in shipping a kit to the nation's capital when you would do just as well to send it to a neighbor.

With circulation shooting beyond the two million mark, *USA Today* should figure into any campaign.

Newsweek
"My Turn"
444 Madison Ave.
New York, NY 10020

Imagine how impressed the relatives will be when, at the Thanksgiving dinner table, you announce that *Newsweek* will soon be carrying your by-lined commentary in "My Turn," a column that accepts material from "anyone and everyone," according to Director of Communications G. H. Simpson.

"The editors look for stories that are personal yet representative of the experiences and feelings of our readers at large. Naturally, better-written stories grab the attention, yet the editors don't shy away from helping My Turners who aren't skilled writers if they have a compelling story to tell."

No subject is off limits, but you're better off with specific, personal issues. If you're mad at the government for deregulating airlines, it probably won't get you into "My Turn." But if you feel you nearly lost your life a couple of times when deregulation prompted TWA to stop serving your community in favor of a regional carrier called Honest John's Airline and Used Car Dealership, you're closer to what the editors need.

"Because of the volume of submissions," says Simpson, "the review process is somewhat lengthy, but eventually all are considered."

26
Publicity at Work

"The public be damned," said Cornelius Vanderbilt at the height of publicity's sleaziest hour. Between 1865 and 1900, when Vanderbilt expressed that touching sentiment, the railroad interests spearheaded a movement to use the press as a vehicle to gain support for their expansion. Truth was not considered an especially useful commodity, especially when an editor might be induced to juggle the facts for, say, two hundred dollars.

Enter the Muckrakers, a group of reformist writers whose ranks included Upton Sinclair, Ida Tarbel, and Lincoln Steffens. They used their skills to further favored causes of their own, usually at odds with the industrialists. Sinclair's *The Jungle*, for example, exposed the horrors of the Chicago stockyards and stands as a sound historical example of persuasion's just side.

The early twentieth century introduced Ivy Lee, a gifted and influential publicist whose work gained him folklore status even in his own time. Lee, who represented John D. Rockefeller, crusaded for a policy of industry keeping the public informed, a rather canny but startling posture in the Robber Baron era. His 1906 lobbying to the press on behalf of the Anthracite Coal Mine Owners, and a much commented upon "statement of principles" released that same year, portrayed his clients as tough but paternalistic architects of an era that would make America great.

Conditions in coal mines were treacherous, and it did occur to many that something was wrong with putting children to work full-time in the sweatshops, but romantic reveries associated with that period of "rugged individualism" persist, thanks in part to Ivy Lee. He was also our century's premier image consultant, changing public perception of Rockefeller from tyrant to a twinkly grandfather figure who had a shiny dime for every kid who crossed his path.

Propaganda was an innocuous word used to describe the flow of information until after World War I when the Allied nations fought with the Germans to influence world opinion. In 1917, the U.S. Committee on Public Information was set up by Congress under the leadership of George Creel. Ideas, it was postulated, are weapons. In the same way that it is difficult to look at a yellowed photograph of a great-grandparent and feel the personality of a long-dead human being, it is hard to imagine the enormity of this assumption. Sure, philosophers said it for centuries, but now a Congressional Committee was meeting to use words like "nerve gas." A few opening shots from our side:

"The war to end war."
"The war to make the world safe for democracy." (We're *still* selling military deployment with that one.)

This was, of course, pabulum compared with what the Nazis, Fascists, and Communists were up to between 1939 and 1941 when they proved to the world that keeping up with the propaganda Joneses was an imperative. Every country scrambled to beef up its internal public-relations apparatus.

In business, we were also learning a few tricks. Shortly after

World War I, Elliott White Springs, a former Air Corps ace, caused widespread controversy when he developed a print advertisement for his line of Spring Maid Sheets. An Indian maiden was pictured on a bed in a desert. In the background, a brave looked very satisfied. The cutline:

"A buck well spent on a Spring Maid Sheet."

Aside from the obvious breakthrough of the effectiveness of sex appeal in advertising, Springs conveyed a couple of important publicity lessons:

1. All successful publicity is ultimately transmitted by word of mouth.

2. An ad can be used to start a publicity campaign.

Radio was booming during this period. Every manufacturer fought for its share of the market and attempted to convince the customer that all radios were not alike. General Electric's Clyde Waggoner arranged for the weekly broadcast of a radio program from the South Pole by Admiral Byrd himself, making sure the world knew that GE and its excellent equipment had orchestrated this superior feat of technology.

Publicity and public relations boomed between world wars. Businesses, emaciated by the Depression, hired consultants to bolster impoverished images, while movie studios, theatrical producers, radio, and other enterprises drummed up business in the heyday of the stunt. Thumb through any newsmagazine of the period and you'll find flagpole sittings, high-wire acts, skywriting, contests of every type, exhibits, and many other gimmicks pegged to specific promotional causes.

Radio programs were named after a sponsor, and the product had a way of appearing throughout the show. Rudy Vallee hosted *The Fleischman Hour*, while Edgar Bergen and Charlie

McCarthy's Sunday night program was known as *The Chase and Sanborn Hour*. Bromo Quinine was as much a part of the Sherlock Holmes adventures as Dr. Watson. Performers plugged their shows with appearances on other programs, a practice that continues today. Fred Allen and Jack Benny met on the air for a March 14, 1937, "feud" designed to publicize their respective network radio shows. This mock battle froze the nation with one of the largest audiences in radio history, second only to one of President Roosevelt's "Fireside Chats." Roosevelt used the power of radio to sell his New Deal programs and soothe a nation suddenly out of work.

Unfortunately, the power of radio did not go unnoticed by any number of fortune tellers, bogus physicians, marriage counselors, and other snake-oil hucksters. These con artists would show up in a town, buy a half-hour of radio time, give a superpitch, and invite listeners to attend a lecture or meet them at a prearranged point of sale. Others would simply go on the air, fabricate case histories of miracle cures, and invite people to send in a mere dollar for the elixir that would do it all. John Romulus Brinkley, the "goat gland man," was typical of the genre that inspired the Communications Act of 1934, when the FCC was born.

Demagogues found pure gold in those airwaves. Father Charles E. Coughlin, a Michigan priest and outspoken social critic, spoke to CBS audiences of 30 to 45 million a week and drew no fewer than 50,000 weekly letters into his Shrine of the Little Flower in Royal Oak. When CBS demanded the right to read his text before letting him on the air, he simply set up his own network with the contributions he received. He'd have loved today's communications satellites.

Columnists dominated. A mention on Walter Winchell's Sunday night radio broadcast ("Good evening Mr. and Mrs. America and all the ships at sea . . .") was supposedly enough, all by itself, to make a book a best seller. A "publicity story" in Hollywood parlance came to mean a piece fabricated for fans.

Stars often went out on dates purely for the benefit of fan magazines and photographers. A contract player about to break
through was given the "publicity treatment" by the studio,
meaning a flood of stories would be sent out and accepted by
the press as truth. Sometimes it was, sometimes it wasn't.
Image was far more important than fact. It's nice to think of
Lana Turner sipping her ice-cream soda at Schwab's, because
the story implies that we can all go there and maybe absorb a
little pixie dust. In reality, Miss Turner became a star through
the less glamorous system of struggling for studio attention to
her talents.

There were also "rumor mills" for word-of-mouth publicity.
These were specialized publicity firms that clients hired to
start rumors about their companies, or, on the dark side that
eventually rendered them illegal, to start talking negatively
and falsely about the competition. Practitioners of this black
art would walk into crowds in pairs and start talking loudly.
Sometimes it took and sometimes it bombed, but the company
always got paid well.

The following cases represent a cross-section of publicity
successes. Most don't include the long shot of national exposure. We know that the *Donahue* show is said to have replaced
Winchell as the book publicist's premier goal, that Don Hewitt
of *Sixty Minutes* has a seventeen-year history of seeing his show
instrumental in getting people into and out of trouble, that
Tonight is the place to open a movie campaign, and that *The
New York Times* can still close a play. But most publicity campaigns don't get that far, and, believe it or not, some aren't
supposed to under any circumstances.

Some who refuse a *Sixty Minutes* interview simply don't
want the world to know how easily they got rich, because by
Monday a lot of sharpies will be on the trail of their market.
They're just as happy publicizing in a region they can control.
Whether you go national or remain in your own area, success
comes with tenacity and a touch of innovation.

PRESS AGENTRY: THE "DISCOVERY" OF EDDIE FISHER

Labor Day weekend is the big one at all Catskills resorts, especially at Grossinger's, the king of the mountains. In 1948, superstar Eddie Cantor discovered a seventeen-year-old singer named Eddie Fisher. The kid got up, sang with the band, and so impressed the headliner that he offered to take the young man on tour if the audience applauded enthusiastically. The response about took the roof off the resort; Fisher went on tour and soon became the heartthrob of the early fifties. The customers loved it and probably remember the event fondly when they take their grandchildren to a *Star Wars* movie starring Fisher's daughter, Carrie. The press ate it up.

New York publicist Tania Grossinger, author of *Growing Up at Grossinger's*, remembers the tale a little differently.

"What really happened," she says, "is that it was worked out months in advance. The kids who lived at the hotel, of which I was one, were told to come to the show—which was very unusual—and fan out all over the room. When Eddie Cantor asked for applause, we were to make a lot of enthusiastic noise. The place went wild."

It might even work today. Eddie Fisher had been spotted as a major young talent and was given a springboard. Would he have made it without that event? Of course. He already had. This "publicity story" was the East Coast equivalent of Lana Turner at Schwab's.

In the mid- or late fifties, Eddie would have been booked on *American Bandstand* or *The Ed Sullivan Show*. Today, his promoters would first ensure that a video got accepted by MTV. If they turned it down, another might be made. Then, you would see him on the musical segment of *Saturday Night Live*, and all over late-night weekend television, either in concert or on video. He might do *Late Night* with David Letterman or *People* magazine. In any case, the process would be comparable to Eddie Fisher's 1948 tour except for the inauthentic stunt. The campaign would be "more honest," but the principles of, and need for, a buildup never change.

THE FEMININE MYSTIQUE: ANOTHER KIND OF BUILDUP

Fifteen years later, Tania Grossinger participated in a publicity campaign where success may have dramatically altered our culture. Ms. Grossinger first worked with Betty Friedan when *McCall's* magazine published excerpts of *The Feminine Mystique*. She was later hired by W. W. Norton, the publisher of the book, to launch a campaign.

Any publicist knows that an important idea can easily go without its proper media attention, and in 1963 the world wasn't exactly begging for its first look at the modern Women's Movement. It is also axiomatic that really revolutionary ideas become publicized through odd combinations of events. In this case, Ms. Grossinger's former position as a *Playboy* publicist had gained her access to the production staff of *The Merv Griffin Show*, then in syndication as the nation's number-one daytime talk show.

"When Merv lost his NBC show and went off the air for a year and a half, I kept in touch. People come and go in this business, and in publicity you try to develop an instinct for those who will be back. It was easy to like the Griffin show people. I made sure that they continued to receive advance copies of the magazine delivered by messenger to them at home. They remembered the courtesy."

Ms. Grossinger recalls that even Merv himself was involved in the Betty Friedan booking. They all sensed the importance of the topic, but they were in an era that did not welcome boat-rocking ideas. These were not the sixties of Abbie Hoffman and Spiro Agnew but the pre-Beatle, New Frontier sixties, a time when career women were often regarded as incomplete souls who somehow blew it and couldn't catch a man. The *Griffin Show* took a chance and booked it.

Next came a program called *Girl Talk* with Virginia Graham.

"Needless to say, Betty took great issue with the title of that show," says Tania Grossinger. "She was always a hard worker who was willing to make every appearance possible to tell people about her book. If there were ten listeners to a radio station, she would be willing to go. That's why she succeeded. It was never handed to her."

Virginia Graham's production people were cool toward the idea. Ms. Grossinger told producer Monte Hill that his host and her client would not get along on the air but that it would be the most memorable segment of *Girl Talk* produced to date. They didn't and it was.

Next came the road. Today, tour information is available from your nearest library, but the publicist of the early sixties had to scratch around to find the best bookings. Ms. Grossinger visited daily an out-of-town newspaper stand on Times Square and ordered copies of *The Seattle Post-Intelligencer*, the *Los Angeles Times*, the *Chicago Tribune*, and others. Her goal was to scan the radio-TV pages and note the listings. She would then check with friends in the cities Ms. Friedan was to visit to discuss the quality of the programs. To further ensure a solid understanding of her interviewers, the author would arrive in a city a day ahead of time to check out as many of her scheduled programs as possible.

Again, would *The Feminine Mystique* have succeeded without the buildup? Its time was certainly right, and history has shown the book to have had enough substance to ensure a strong word of mouth. Without these qualities, nothing can sell. And, as Ms. Grossinger is quick to point out, the ultimate credit in a campaign goes to the person in front of the camera. Only she can finally do the selling. But the Eddie Fisher discovery and the behind-the-scenes work on *The Feminine Mystique* serve to illustrate a very important publicity lesson. Nothing gets done if you wait around the soda fountain of your own corner drugstore and hope that a talent scout will happen by.

NEW ROCHELLE, NEW YORK, AND A BOOK THAT IMPROVED ITS IMAGE

New Rochelle, New York, was experiencing a familiar pattern of urban blight in its downtown area. The city of 70,000, though not going to seed, did need to beef up its visibility to compete with other Westchester County communities for new industries and residents.

First a number of citizens' volunteer task forces were set up at the urging of New York's prestigious public-relations consulting firm Ruder and Finn. One of these groups spent three years developing a 224-page hardcover book of photographs called *New Rochelle: Portrait of a City.*

The New Rochelle Development Council, a nonprofit group consisting of sixty blue-ribbon members of the city's corporate community, raised $10,000 to cover the initial publication costs. Once the book became available, a special advance discount was made available with much success.

A thousand posters trumpeting the book's existence were distributed throughout the community. An exhibit of its photographs was displayed in the public library and other locations, including a fair attended by thousands of Westchester County residents. The Chamber of Commerce got involved, and soon businesses were offering the books for sale. Real-estate brokers offered it free to prospects looking to settle in New Rochelle.

Opera star and longtime New Rochelle resident Robert Merrill took the cause to the airwaves of *Live at Five*, a celebrity-studded local news program on WNBC-TV in New York. The appearance resulted in orders from throughout New York, New Jersey, and Connecticut. Within two months, the book had sold 1,500 copies, a remarkable number for a $25 book on sale in a single community. It continues to sell and to act as a quiet but effective booster for the community. More important, the project rallied the residents around the cause of civic pride.

JORDACHE: MAKING THE OLD PIZAZZ WORK IN MODERN TIMES

When New York lost its lights during the summer of 1977, Joe, Ralph, and Avi Nakash lost their Brooklyn jeans shop to vandals. When the insurance money came through, they decided to manufacture their own jeans. They combined letters in their names with a little *che* at the end for a touch of French (French jeans dominated the designer-jeans marketplace at the time), and set out to sell Jordache jeans.

With an entrepreneurial panache that is rarely seen in these cautious times, they decided to risk everything by investing in commercial time on *Sixty Minutes*. Their ad, however, featured a topless woman riding a horse and proved to be too suggestive for CBS. They hired New York public-relations consultant J. Wilfred Gagen and began a romance with the press that would soon help elevate them to the top spot in their marketplace. The *Sixty Minutes* rejection played extremely well, and when *The New York Times* made them reshoot a similar topless ad because the models were smiling, Gagen quipped, "We have come to the inexorable conclusion that the morality of *The New York Times* is that you can do whatever you want as long as you don't enjoy it." More coverage. Meanwhile, Ralph Nakash came up with the concept of the "Jordache Look" and reinforced the exclusivity by limiting the manufacture of the product to size 36 and below.

The company that knocked *The Times* could also take a joke. In fact, the more jokes the better. *Saturday Night Live* did a parody as did *Fridays*, its counterpart on ABC. Every comic in every club seemed to have at least one "Jordache

Look" joke. A major break for the company came when the ultimate jokester, Johnny Carson, began to include the product's name regularly in his opening monologue.

Jordache wasn't bashful about staging an event in the form of a Jordache Blimp. When it crashed on takeoff, however (no one was hurt), the evening was in danger of fizzling until the company rushed models to the scene in ambulances. Everyone had a party, and there was more coverage.

Jordache people were also smart enough to make hay with their most serious theft problem, counterfeiting. Gone were the jokes as detectives closed in on bogus Jordache distributors. The press was sometimes invited to go on the raids. The counterfeiting may have been a serious threat, but the coverage continued.

Publicity alone didn't do it for Jordache, but it certainly has to have been instrumental in making one company name synonymous with the designer-jean craze that will always be a prevailing image when one remembers the early eighties.

ALLSTATE: YOU'RE IN GOOD HANDS WITH A FILM

When Allstate Insurance began campaigning for standardization of air bags in American cars, they commenced an uphill climb that continues today. But their name has been associated with this cause since 1971, a fact which prompted the production manager of a film company to contact them for assistance in creating a crash scene in *Moving Violation,* a feature film released by Twentieth Century-Fox. Would they provide two cars equipped with air bags? They would, but with a few stipulations.

Jack Martens, Allstate's automotive engineering director, would have to be technical adviser and director of the crash scene. After much vigorous bargaining, the company got its way. One can only imagine the sessions when an insurance company was demanding to direct the most dangerous car stunt in film history. And it *was* dangerous.

The scene called for a 1974 Oldsmobile to crash into a concrete wall at more than thirty miles per hour. We're talking about the certainty of death here. If you tried it without an air bag, you would never live through it. The stunt man at first refused to go anywhere near such a preposterous scheme. Ultimately, the car hit the wall at 32.6 miles per hour, and Allstate's version of the footage was turned into a short subject called *Ridin' the Edge*. It drew applause at its Radio City Music Hall premier in November of 1976 and continued to do so throughout its accompanying run with such hits as *Smokey and the Bandit, Smokey and the Bandit II*, and *Hooper*. It was also distributed to television and cable. By 1980, *Ridin' the Edge* had been seen 125,633 times by 46 million people. Opinion-research polls conducted by the company indicated that positive attitudes toward air bags had swelled by 27 percent during the first four years of release. It's still drawing applause.

A SATELLITE STORY

When the Canadian government wanted to publicize its contribution to America's space program, it undertook the production of a three-part news feature timed to be released by satellite to American television news directors prior to the launch of the *Columbia* space shuttle in 1982. The feature received a pickup by 100 network affiliates with an estimated audience of 6 million viewers.

BETHLEHEM STEEL'S LETTER TO THE PRESIDENT

When Elliott White Springs ran his Indian maiden ad and profited from the resulting publicity, he certainly never would have imagined that his pairing of advertising and publicity would one day be practiced by a major steel company in the cause of energy conservation. In 1977, Bethlehem Steel ran a series of advertisements in *Time, Newsweek, U.S. News and World Report, The Wall Street Journal,* and *Sports Illustrated.* The message was simple:

> Time is running out. Tell President Carter what you think he should do about energy.

A page was left blank for readers to write a letter to the President of the United States. The President and members of Congress received thousands of these letters, and hundreds more were sent to Bethlehem's headquarters thanking them for "doing something" about the energy problem. Maybe they did.

TAKING PUBLICITY TO TELEVISION

With the emergence of economical cable channels and satellite transponders, all of us can take our pitch to the video revolution. But Theodore H. Pincus, president of the Financial Relations Board of Chicago, didn't have such gadgets in 1971 when he sought a means of publicizing his firm and its clients.

Pincus approached WCIU-TV, a UHF station that beamed most of its programs toward the financial community. The result was *Industries of the Seventies,* a panel discussion program that usually aired live at the close of the stock market. Its purpose was twofold: exposure and the transmission of useful information.

Every week there was a debate, usually between top corporate executives (including the CEO where possible) and securities analysts specializing in their industries. The WCIU-TV audience was small, but Pincus wasn't trying to produce *Search for Tomorrow.* He wanted to reach the financial community and did so. The program drew rave reviews, especially from registered brokers who found the input of corporation management valuable in their work.

Industries of the Seventies was an early example of narrowcasting, and an extraordinarily successful one.

THE AC TRANSIT COMPANY AND THE SELLING OF A NUISANCE

In the late sixties, drivers aboard the buses of San Francisco's AC Transit Company were facing extraordinary danger as their fare boxes became collection plates for street thugs. When a driver was shot and nearly killed during a robbery, the publicity prompted officials to take quick action. In fact, the AC public-relations department was given a month to implement a plan to sell reluctant passengers who used the buses 52 million times each year on a program of prepayment. The rapid-fire transition, which stands as a textbook success in getting people to buy an inconvenience, went roughly as follows:

- Everything's in a name, and the first accomplishment was to come up with one that worked. They called it "Ready Fare" and began making a lot of clamor about "RF Day," when the drivers would be free of their fare boxes.

- Those who argued that it was inconvenient to carry exact change and a real nuisance if you got on the bus and discovered that you didn't have it were stopped in their tracks by a program whereby the drivers would accept up to $5, deposit it into a locked box, and issue the passenger a scrip that could be used for future trips.

- Outside ticket booths were set up with an introductory offer: buy four tickets and get one free.

- New ticket books were issued in appealing pastels.

- Press releases blanketed the media, reporting on progress.

- Public-service announcements ran on radio and television; newspapers endorsed the effort with editorials.

- Businesses chipped in and sold tickets while the program was getting under way.

- A staged delivery of new tokens by armored car drew coverage on the evening news.

- The Chamber of Commerce did a mailing.

- Television covered the turning in of the fare boxes, and all media paid proper attention to the "RF Day" plan where smiling drivers, including the now recovered holdup victim, endorsed the plan.

Today, it is an article of faith that bus drivers in large cities simply do not make change. But in 1969, the concept was new, and one must applaud those overworked PR people for pulling the whole plan together.

THE SOLO SINGING DOG CONTEST

In 1975, Wayne Pet Foods, a successful processor of food for laboratory and veterinary purposes, decided to enter the commercial dog food market with their product, Solo. Their commercials featured dogs singing, naturally, "O Solo Mio." Because they wanted to go beyond advertising, they contracted the New York-based firm of Burson-Marsteller, one of the world's largest public-relations firms. Those who knock the big PR firms as stuffy, take note.

Burson's solution was a series of contests for singing dogs. They would enter a market and hold auditions that were announced by small ads and column-item publicity. These sessions must have been something to remember, especially if they were conducted by Burson-Marsteller executives, who groom and dress with a sartorial perfection that makes most bankers look like Bowery drunks. A key attraction was a singing dog named Candy who had performed to thunderous applause on the *Tonight Show*.

Not only were Candy and her trainer, Ed Boulton, booked on local shows in twelve cities, but a staff spokesman was trained to talk about training dogs to sing Solo.

To test the effectiveness of the campaign, two markets of comparable size, Albany and Wichita, were saturated with advertising and the usual sales-promotion material for Solo. But Wichita had the added hoopla of the publicity. In Albany, research revealed that postadvertising product awareness came in at the expected 30 percent level. But in Wichita, with the singing dogs and the local appearances, postadvertising awareness rose to 60 percent.

Researched publicity campaigns are tabulated in impressions, or the number of times the product is syringed into people's thought processes. The twelve-city tour produced 50 million impressions, while exposure on NBC, ABC, TVN, a syndicated television news feature service, and the front page of *The Wall Street Journal* generated somewhere between 75 and 100 million additional impressions. That's pretty serious underscoring to a supposedly frivolous campaign.

27

Directories: Your Real Contacts

Start with a visit to your local library and browse through the reference rooms, checking every directory in residence. There's even a *Directory of Directories*. You don't have to even touch them; just know how many exist and form a rough idea of what they do.

Most of us don't have the patience to endure the initial disorientation of a library. We're action people, accustomed to defining a problem and getting on with it. Thumbing through weatherbeaten card catalogues and volumes of esoteric books is, for many, not unlike having to make friends with a foreigner who speaks a dialect comprehensible only to a few tribe members on the other side of the world.

You don't need a network of high-powered media contacts to garner a million dollars' worth of publicity, but you do need reference texts. Even the smallest public library offers some of these volumes, and it can usually procure others for you if it is connected to a regional library system. Even if you have to drive a half-hour to a larger library, the trip will be worth it. If you are planning a tour, or any large-scale regional campaign, the purchase of one or two of these books is highly recommended.

Reference books are your uncle in the business. They name names, cite audience and circulation figures, provide the technical specs of radio and television stations, and offer a variety of booking guidelines. *News at Noon* is live; *Perspective* tapes on Wednesdays; don't send materials to the station but to the home of the producer. The books are very much like automobiles in that each has a feel, a mood, a suitability to your temperament. Some publicists would rather have surgery than attempt a campaign without Larami. Others regard N. W. Ayer or Richard Weiner as part of the office staff. Broadcasters who become publicists feel naked without the *Broadcasting/Cablecasting Yearbook*. Nearly everyone stocks the *Editor & Publisher Yearbook* for newspaper booking.

There are no rights or wrongs, except that it is an immoral waste of time to attempt a campaign without some of these texts. Browse, test-drive, and choose for yourself. They're all excellent. If you see one that appears to be a "must" and your library can't get it for you, write to the publisher and ask for promotional literature that includes sample listings. You're going after tens of thousands of dollars in free exposure. If you have to invest $50 in the one directory that saves weeks of time, you'll have spent wisely.

Ayer Public Relations and Publicity Style Book
426 Pennsylvania Ave.
Fort Washington, PA 19034

(There is an Ayer directory for every publicity purpose under heaven. The same holds true for Larami, Weiner, Lesly, O'Dwyer, PR Aids, and others, so don't stop here.)

Bacon's Publicity Checker
Bacon's Publishing Company, Inc.
332 South Michigan Ave.
Chicago, Il 60604

(Did you know that there is a publication called *Bus Ride*? It reaches 12,500 bus transportation executives and can be found in Spokane, Washington, according to *Bacon's*, which also lists the editor's name and telephone number. *Muffler Digest?* Easy. See page 32.)

Broadcasting/Cablecasting Yearbook
1735 De Sales St. NW
Washington, DC 20036

(No radio station, cable system, or television station escapes being listed in this useful starter publication. When you're doing your first pitch to local public-affairs and news shows, this one is invaluable. It won't help you much for major-market talk shows.)

Cable Advertising Directory
Cabletelevision Advertising Bureau
National Cable Television Association
1724 Massachusetts Ave. NW
Washington, DC 20036

(Everything you need to know about local cable systems, who operates them, what satellite services they provide, and how much advertising time is worth. If you plan a truly extensive cable campaign that includes the new networks, write to NCTA and find out where the updated literature can be found. Cable goes up and down like the stock market and changes dramatically from year to year.)

Handbook of Public Relations
McGraw-Hill Book Company
1221 Ave. of the Americas
New York, NY 10020

Larami Communications Associates
151 East 50th St.
New York, NY 10022

(Publishes computerized updates on its very comprehensive *Cable Contacts*, *Television Contacts*, and *Radio Contacts*.)

New York Publicity Outlets
Washington Depot, CT 06794

(No one books New York without this publication. It doesn't make the Apple any easier to book; it merely makes it *possible*. Also publishers of *TV Publicity Outlets* and the *Cable Contacts Yearbook*.)

Hotel & Motel Red Book
American Hotel Association Directory Corporation
888 Seventh Ave.
New York, NY 10019

Official Airline Guide
2000 Clearwater Dr.
Oak Brook, IL 60521

National Radio Publicity Director
National Television Publicity Directory
Peter Glenn Publications
17 East 48th St.
New York, NY 10017

Lesly's Public Relations Handbook
Prentice-Hall, Inc.
Englewood Cliffs, NJ 07632

Encyclopedia of Business Information Sources
Gale Research Company
Book Tower
Detroit, MI 48226

Practical Handbook of Public Relations
by Robert S. Cole
Prentice-Hall, Inc.
Englewood Cliffs, NJ 07632

Professional's Guide to Publicity
by Richard Weiner
Public Relations Publishing
888 Seventh Ave.
New York, NY 10019

Public Relations Information Sources
Management Information Guide #22
by Alice Norton
Gale Research Company
Book Tower
Detroit, MI 48226

Directory of Personal Image Consultants
Editorial Services Company
1140 Ave. of the Americas
New York, NY 10036

O'Dwyer's Directory of Corporate Communications
O'Dwyer's Directory of Public Relations Firms
J. R. O'Dwyer Company Inc.
271 Madison Ave.
New York, NY 10016

PR Aids Party Line
221 Park Ave. South
New York, NY 10003

United States Publicity Directory
National Register Publishing Company Inc.
20 East 46th St.
New York, NY 10017

TV Publicity Outlets
Washington Depot, CT 06794

Working Press of the Nation
National Research Bureau Inc.

(National Research Bureau also publishes a valuable *Annual Talk Show Directory.*)

Editor & Publisher Yearbook
575 Lexington Ave.
New York, NY 10022

Hudson's Washington News Media Contacts
2926 Pennsylvania Ave. NW
Washington, DC 20037

Magazine Industry Marketplace
Literary Market Place
R.R. Bowker Company
P.O. Box 1807
Ann Arbor, MI 48106

(Good if you plan to actually write and place an article as a publicity mechanism, or if you want to follow the City of New Rochelle's example and contract to have a book published.)

Bibliography

Binder, Amy. "Renewal of New Rochelle: A Public Relations Case Study," *Public Relations Journal*, Vol. 38, No. 3, March 1982.

Chapman, Ray. "Measurement: Alive and Well," *Public Relations Journal*, Vol. 38, No. 5, May 1982.

Endicott, W. P. "Business News Goes on the Air," *Public Relations Journal*, Vol. 26, No. 4, April 1970.

Grossinger, Tania. *Growing Up at Grossinger's*. New York: David McKay, 1975.

Klepper, Michael M. "News Releases Go into Orbit," *Public Relations Journal*, Vol. 38, No. 8, August 1982.

Langley, Edward. "Panache at Jordache," *Public Relations Journal*, Vol. 38, No. 8, August 1982.

Lewis, David. "The Outstanding PR Professionals," *Public Relations Journal*, Vol. 26, No. 10, October 1970.

O'Connor, Dennis. "Inconvenience Can Be Sold," *Public Relations Journal*, Vol. 25, No. 1, January 1969.

Pincus, Theodore H. "Using TV in Financial Relations: Case History of a Sponsored Program," *Public Relations Journal*, Vol. 27, No. 4, April 1971.

Suell, Richard W. "When Management Meets the Press," *Public Relations Journal*, Vol. 27, No. 1, January 1971.

Index

235